EXCERPT Magazine No. 1
Copyright ©2023
ISBN: 978-0-9855180-3-5
www.excerptmag.com

Excerpts from *The Vacation* (Expat Press, 2022),
Pure Cosmos Club (Stalking Horse Press, May 2023),
The Moth for the Star (7.13 Books, September 2023)
printed with permission from the presses.

Editor's Note

Dear Reader,

You are about to embark on a journey into eight fictive dreams—novel excerpts from emerging writers with unpublished manuscripts or books recently/soon-to-be-published from independent presses. You will travel from New York and Los Angeles to London, the pyramids of Egypt, former West Berlin, the Florida wilds, out to sea on a bizarre cruise and into the safe haven of a speculative city of secrets.

We could pontificate on the import of these excerpts—how they hold enduring insights on the human experience that will somehow cure world hunger, save our planet, and better society through the characters' trials and triumphs, their folly and wisdom. But we won't. They are stories, just stories. That's enough. And maybe you will awake from the dream with a vague hopeful feeling that we are all messy humans in a very messy world and that's a beautiful miraculous thing indeed. We are the stories we tell ourselves after all—who we are, who we were, who we want to be.

We're proud to publish excerpts from these emerging novelists (all unagented *wink*) and hope you enjoy the first issue.

All the best,

DW Ardern
Editor-in-Chief

*

EXCERPT MAGAZINE

No. 1   Spring 2023

In This Issue

Masthead

DW Ardern   Editor-in-Chief
Jenny Maattala   Fiction Editor
Cam Terwilliget   Fiction Editor
Isaac High   Assistant Editor
Justin Richel   Cover Artist

PURE COSMOS CLUB

by

MATTHEW BINDER

CHAPTER 1

Today, Janie is picking up the furniture she left when she moved out. Her text last week was our first contact since the incident at the park back in April. It's true I may have been out of sorts, but I don't remember behaving as she claims. I was only there to give her a birthday present, the manhole cover I'd stolen off the street and painted to look like Io, the innermost of the four moons round the planet Jupiter. Years before, on our second date, we'd visited the planetarium. Janie had gazed up teary-eyed at the artificial sky and said Io was the most exquisite object in all the universe. To this day, I can't understand why she called the cops.

She's supposed to be here in twenty minutes, which means I should expect her in ten. She's always said punctuality is one of the five keys to unlocking our true potential. I can't recall the other four, but they must be working for her. She's recently taken a lucrative position at a dermatology clinic in SoHo.

I've been in bed playing my favorite game with Blanche. I lie with my eyes closed and arms folded across my chest, holding my breath, trying to convince her I've passed away. It takes all my self-control to stifle a giggle when she licks my ear.

She entered my life when I took a shortcut through a dark alley on my bike and hit her. The vet said her two hind legs were permanently damaged and recommended euthanasia. Instead, I built a contraption from the wheels of a tricycle. Blanche took to it immediately, of course, and now she scoots through the apartment at top speed.

I don't mean to say our relationship has been without hardship. The day I brought her home, she relieved herself on my favorite jacket. I've recently discovered, moreover, that I'm allergic to her dander and so I am always sleepy from taking antihistamines.

When I can't contain myself any longer and gasp for breath, Blanche goes berserk, bouncing up and down on her front legs, while her bad ones lie behind like overcooked spaghetti. I sweep her into my arms and give her a few pats on the head and a rub behind her ears.

It's not until the buzzer sounds that I realize the apartment's condition has deteriorated in Janie's absence. A black mold has crept across the ceiling, and laundry, dirty dishes, and art supplies are strewn everywhere. More disconcerting, when did this odor first appear? There's a knock on the door. I glance in the mirror. My hair is standing straight up. I lick my palm and try to pat it down, but it's no use.

"Go easy on her, Paul," I think. "It must be hard enough for her already, having so many bad marks in God's account ledger."

Two men are at the door, one black and one white. They have thick necks and smooth, handsome faces. Blanche drags herself over and growls. The white guy bends down to pet her, and she bares her teeth.

"Now, Blanche," I say. "Mind your manners."

"Her name is Blanche?" the black guy says.

"The only name fitting for such a distinguished lady."

"Like from *A Streetcar Named Desire*?" the white guy says.

"Can I help you gentlemen?"

"We're here to pick up Janie's things," the white guy says.

"Where is she?"

"Downstairs."

"I'd like to speak with her."

"She'd prefer you didn't," the black guy says.

I bow my head and let them in. They lift the couch, exposing broken paintbrushes, a half-eaten grilled cheese sandwich, the shattered remains of an ant farm, a broken Rolex watch given to me by my grandfather upon completing a scuba diving certification at the local YMCA (the highest level of educational achievement I've attained), and a collection of baby teeth in a Ziplock bag I've held onto since boyhood. The men move with ease and grace. Their voices—much richer and deeper than mine—echo off the walls as they discuss how to navigate the stairs. I gaze out the window. Across the parking lot, Janie opens the back of a U-Haul. In yoga pants and a sweatshirt, she moves effortlessly, like a swan across a lake. I unwrap a package of strawberry Pop-Tarts—one for each of us, Blanche and me. The men return and point to a painting of a horse jumping a fence, one of the first I made for Janie.

"She said we should take the horse painting too," the white guy says.

"I don't have much use," I say, "for old paintings, furniture, lamps, rugs, these kinds of things."

The black guy hoists the bookcase onto his shoulder, while the white guy takes the painting. I close the door and return to the window. The men place my things in the truck. Janie gives the white guy a high-five. Then the black guy takes Janie in his arms for a rather intimate kiss. When Janie catches me watching from the window, she looks away quickly and jumps into the truck.

A stack of books against the wall falls into another, which falls into another yet. Everything is everywhere. I sit in the middle of it and let Blanche lick my face.

Chapter 2

The sky is overcast and the air hot and sticky as I make my daily walk to the warehouse where I rent studio space from my friend, Danny. I stay on the shady side of the street, but there's no escaping the heat. Sweat stings my eyes. Already, my face is burned.

A long time ago, I read in an etiquette book that a gentleman never wears shorts unless he's exercising or at the beach. My adherence to this rule is absolute, even as the temperature nears a hundred degrees. When I was a boy, my father told me I have unsightly legs. My knees, he said, were knobbier than a dresser full of drawers. His words left an indelible mark, and now, even while bathing, I make sure to keep my knees covered by a washcloth. A rash has formed where my jeans rub my thighs, so every few steps I have to adjust myself. The farther I walk, the harder it becomes. Poor Blanche is weary of my incessant complaints. Two men pass, dressed in floral shorts and tank tops. I can't help but envy their pragmatic sensibilities.

Back when Danny bought the warehouse from a retired mechanic who used it as a chop-shop for stolen BMWs, the neighborhood was a colorful place, where one constantly found oneself embroiled in all manner of adventure. A stray bullet once shattered the studio's window and put a hole through the canvas I was painting. Another time, I was held up at knifepoint over a box of pork buns. Danny always insisted the building was a prodigious investment, but years later, here we are, and I'm sorry to report he was wrong. Real estate prices have skyrocketed, forcing out the pawn shop where I once got a tremendous deal on a gold chain and the liquor store that sold loosie cigarettes for a quarter. In their places are a vegan cheese shop and a florist that specializes in lesbian weddings.

For months, I've pleaded with Danny to use his connections to help me get my work seen. But he's always refused, claiming not to want any part in subjecting the public to my "perverted worldview." My work, Danny says, epitomizes everything he hates in art, namely that it takes into account supernatural forces.

"Religion is dead," he once said, "but your provincial superstitions remain."

Nevertheless, he's recently experienced a change of heart.

"At the very least you never bore me," Danny said last week, then told me he's arranged for one of my pieces to be included at a group show organized by his gallerist, Susan.

The thing I admire most about Danny is that he viciously hates anyone who bores him. The man simply can't distinguish between an evil person and an uninteresting one.

I'd been working on a series of paintings of Gwyneth Paltrow. With each piece, she became more satanic and menacing, until finally she sprouted bat wings and horns, holding all of mankind in a saucer of anti-aging cream. Just as I was almost finished, I sliced my finger opening a can of soup, inspiring me to abandon the project.

Instead, I decided to climb a tree. Halfway up the elm I'd picked—it was especially fine, I thought—a branch snapped, and I fell. It was then I had the vision for the work I'm making now, a sculpture of a baby nailed to a cross constructed of cellphones. The difficulty, of course, has been gathering the phones. After exhausting my resources buying used devices on Craigslist and eBay, I was still nowhere near my goal of the five hundred I absolutely require, so I ran a funding campaign on social media, which, somehow, was met with what I can only call apathy, and, at times, even scorn. This left me with no recourse but to rob a Best Buy recycling center, a move that Blanche and I deemed both courageous and bold. Anticipating the major stir my piece would cause in the art world, I penned an open letter to the noted critic Jerry Saltz, of *New York Magazine*. "I think we can agree, sir," I wrote, "that in this sea of idling conformity, even the smallest act of subversion or rebellion cannot but be heralded as a shining triumph."

Public opinion, I've learned, however, is not my friend. The response to my crime has been so unfavorable that Blanche thinks I should move abroad and change my name. I've been so afraid, in fact, that for the last several days I've lain in bed chewing bubble gum and picturing myself dragged from the show in handcuffs.

Danny's parked his Lamborghini in front of the studio, a replacement for the Maserati he drove into a lake last month. Already he's hard at work in his uniform of camouflage shorts and the tie-dye tank top that shows off the stick-and-poke tattoos he gave himself one night while under the influence of ayahuasca. He's nearly completed his training to become a Sun Dance Chief, studying under a part-Crow, part-Sioux, part-Jew survivalist named Shelley. His final objective is to retrieve the carcasses of four golden eagles.

I don't know how he does these things, but overnight Danny has constructed a ten-foot-long sandbox in the studio in which he's now observing a black and yellow snake. No detail is too minute. Whether the snake slithers, coils, or flicks its tongue, Danny writes a detailed account in his

Moleskine notebook.

"I'm glad you're here," he says at last. "I need your help."

Danny leads me to the alley behind the studio, where a pool of blood has collected on the ground. I flinch at the scene, but Danny seems entirely disaffected.

"They should be about dry now," he says, glancing up. "We need to get them inside before the birds pick them clean."

Overhead, a wire has been strung across the alley from which hang what appear to be furry rugs. Something drips onto my face as I squint—a strange phenomenon, indeed, since there's not a cloud in the sky. It's not rain on the back of my hand, however, but blood.

"They're from roadkill," Danny says, and begins to hand me the hides. "Cats."

I'm struck by the juxtaposition: the empty gleam in the eyes of these dead animals belies their lustrous coats.

"How'd things go with Janie this morning?" he says, gesturing me to follow him back inside, where he fills a garbage can with water and a box of salt.

"She sent two men to collect her stuff."

"It's often difficult to imagine what makes one person attracted to another. I never could understand what she saw in you."

I drop the skins into the water, then go to the sink to rinse my arms. But even before I've touched the faucet, I'm stabbed by something, in my leg. I shriek, and when I look down, Danny's snake is retreating to the radiator.

"Your snake just bit me, Danny."

"You should go to the hospital immediately."

"Is it poisonous?"

"It's an Eastern Coral Snake, one of the deadliest in the world, though they're usually very mild-mannered. You must've done something to provoke it."

My leg is really starting to throb. I roll up my pants to find two perfect red puncture wounds.

"Will you drive me to the hospital?"

"Just give me a minute to tie up some loose ends here."

I open Danny's snake handbook for instructions. The author strongly advises against sucking out the venom or even applying a tourniquet. Ice is also discouraged. Without treatment, I learn, I could be dead in hours.

The studio is always hot this time of year, but never have I sweated like this. A tightness has gripped my chest, I can hardly breathe, and a tingling sensation has spread through my face. My vision is blurry. I'm even drooling on my shirt. In no time at all, I'm overcome by a weepy drowsiness and crash to the floor, barely conscious.

Danny says he needs to finish labeling the animal tracks he cast in plaster earlier in the day. If he doesn't do it now, vital data he collected on his survivalist retreat will be lost. His reputation is at stake, he says, which I suppose is true. Danny has amassed the largest private collection of paw prints on the Eastern seaboard, and his assemblage of marsupial casts is on loan to the Zoology Department at Harvard.

"You doing okay down there?" he says, as Blanche fans her tail in my face.

I laugh like a hysterical child. "It's just melting away," I mutter, "all the suffering!"

Next to my head, I see a fortune cookie that must've fallen off the table where Danny takes his lunch. I manage to crack the cookie open. "You've been dying," the fortune says, "since your first breath." Waiting for Danny to finish, I think of all the time I've wasted treating myself to life's little pleasures with nothing but regrets to show for it.

When I was in the fifth grade, my best friend Jesse and his family moved to Kansas City. Just before they piled into the station wagon, he gave me a story he'd written documenting an adventure the two of us had shared crossing the city of Denver on our bikes. I spent the afternoon hunched in a closet with a flashlight reading it over and over through tear-filled eyes. Jesse told our story with such poignant tenderness that it was difficult to believe it hadn't been a lost classic by Mark Twain. I sobbed uncontrollably at the thought of losing him. He'd been my only friend since first grade, when he was kind enough to swap lunches with me after my mother had packed me a turkey sandwich, knowing very well I was a vegan.

Shortly after Jesse moved, there was a call for entries in a writing competition at my school. I worked hard on a tale about the time I brought home the class's pet salamander for the weekend only to lose him in the creek, yet nothing I wrote could match the eloquence of Jesse. In despair, I copied Jesse's work and submitted it to the contest.

A month later, the entire student body packed into the gymnasium for the quarterly assembly. First, we were forced to endure the marching band's spirited but uneven performance of the school's fight song. Next, the girls' basketball team was honored for their fifth-place finish in the district tournament. Then the vice-principal announced an upcoming carwash fundraiser. Finally, Mr. Mackey, the chair of the school's English Department, delivered a rambling panegyric about the school's depth of talented writers. I left my seat in the bleachers to fetch a Dr. Pepper from the vending machine. When my dollar bill got jammed, I kicked the machine until the custodian, Mateo, raced down the hall waving his arms and shouting. I had won the writing contest, he said. The whole school was waiting for me to accept the prize.

"What about my Dr. Pepper?" I said.

Mateo rocked the machine back and forth, and sodas of all variety came spitting out. "Take whatever you want," he said.

Upon my return, the crowd rose to its feet and exploded with applause. Mr. Mackey shook my hand and introduced me as the greatest writer from Colorado since John Fante. I chugged my entire Dr. Pepper for strength.

"It's a great honor to stand here before you today," I said.

"'Two Bikes, One City' is a tale of friends who don't know how to despair, boys so resolute in their determination to conquer a city that they feel almost humiliated by their own strength of character, boys who were ready to leave behind all they knew, to cut themselves off from the world, like castaways on a desert island, to seek their fortune. I consider myself one of destiny's elect, an adventurer who has triumphed against all odds to write the tale of a generation. Please, when you pass me in these halls, try to think of my accomplishments and be inspired to reach inside yourselves, for it's only there that you'll find the stuff of which you're truly made."

Mr. Mackey started a literary magazine to publish the work. Sales of the story were so strong that the school was able to re-sod the football field. My handwritten copy was placed in a glass vitrine in the administrative offices. Every day I had to walk past it and be reminded of my grift.

Again and again, I promised myself I'd contact Jesse to confess my misdeed, but I always found a reason not to. A year passed before I received news that he had perished in an accident. He had left a note for his mother explaining that he missed his best friend Paul and was riding his bike from Kansas City to Denver to surprise him. Jesse had ridden five hundred and ninety-seven miles of the six-hundred-and-twenty-mile journey when he was struck by a cement truck.

I wake in the hospital with a tube up my nose and a nurse pricking me with a needle. The doctor arrives, and I recognize her immediately as a friend of Janie's. We had met at various social functions Janie had forced me to attend. Her imperious eyes twinkle with misgivings.

"Paul, is that you? What happened?"

"*Tttthnaaaake biiiide.*"

A nurse is sent to retrieve the anti-venom vaccine. It's lucky they have any in stock, Janie's friend explains, as snake-bites are uncommon in Brooklyn. When Janie's friend asks how it is I was bitten, I invent a tale about volunteering at the Bronx Zoo, then feign tiredness and close my eyes.

CHAPTER 3

I've been in the hospital now for two days. The staff has been kind enough to make an exception to their "no pet" rule. A few raindrops fall outside as Blanche and I flip through a stack of gossip magazines given to us by the nurse. We examine a photo of Nick Lachey and his lovely wife, Vanessa, inspecting produce at a farmers' market. The picture's caption is a quote from Nick, reflecting on his fall from celebrity. "One morning I woke up and realized I have my whole life ahead of me!" This bit of hopefulness triggers Blanche's gag reflex, and she spits up on the magazine. If there's one thing Blanche loathes, it's optimism. God knows, out on the streets, she learned that to foresee the worst helps to prepare against it.

I push the button to beckon a nurse for a dose of morphine, which, as these things often do, sends me into yet another bout of dizzying self-reflection.

Eleven months ago, I walked into a meeting at my job to discuss plans for expanding a digital media campaign to new markets. I'd come armed with a number of talking points scribbled on a napkin from the nearby bodega, where I'd just picked up lunch. I was in a tremendous mood after an event that I'd believed was a fortuitous omen.

For lunch, I'd got a falafel sandwich, a Dr. Pepper, and a bag of pistachios. No sooner had I left the place than I dropped the bag of pistachios into a puddle. There was a hole in the packaging, and my pistachios were ruined. I became enraged, certain this tragedy would mar my day. It was then that I remembered I suffer from a terrible pistachio allergy. The last time I ate them my throat had swelled completely shut. The only reason I'm still here, actually, is the kindness of the stranger who stuck me with his EpiPen. Now, once again, I realized, my life had been spared! I was overcome with joy and stood laughing in the crosswalk while drivers honked and shouted. I couldn't understand why it had been so long since I'd last felt this free.

My father was fifty-four when I was born, the product of an ill-conceived fling. Three years prior, despite having never ridden a motorcycle, he bought one on impulse after watching an old Peter Fonda movie, then taught himself to ride in the backyard. A few days later his wife came out to call him for dinner only to see him lose control of the motorcycle and drive it straight into her. The paramedics rushed her to the hospital for a series of radical procedures, but they all failed, and she died three weeks later.

The only thing that kept my father going was his work as a low-level bureaucrat for the municipal agency that managed the city's telephone lines. That was where he met my mother, a thirty-nine-year-old, multiple divorcée who worked part-time as a receptionist. She once told me that what she first noticed about my father was his "tireless appetite for drudgery."

They went out on a handful of dates before my mother broke it off with him because he chewed his fingernails incessantly. A month later, she learned she was pregnant, the outcome of their one sexual encounter—five minutes, she told me, of passionless sex after too many tequila sodas at a happy-hour function. Out of a sense of duty, they married.

More than fifteen years later, I spent my birthday watching reruns of the classic television show CHiPs in which two California Highway Patrol motorcycle officers cruised the freeways of Los Angeles solving crimes. My father came home from work that night to microwave a frozen Salisbury steak. While he waited, he started a letter to the local paper, rebuking them for advertising women's underwear. But before he could finish, the sound of my high-pitched chortle, which he'd repeatedly complained gave him migraines, interrupted him. Only children and perverts laughed, he shouted, nobody else. Now that I was fifteen, he said, my laughter was forbidden.

After all these years, thanks to my mishap with the pistachios, this gift of laughter had been restored, so that when I stepped into the conference room for my meeting, my spirits were high. But instead of the marketing team, I was met by my somber-faced boss and a lady from HR. My boss repeated that though I was a well-liked member of the team, my performance had never met even the minimum expectations. The nice woman from HR handed me a copy of the termination paperwork and said she hoped the two-month severance package they were offering would soften the blow.

It's true I'd never reached my revenue targets. It's difficult even now to explain where I'd gone wrong. Every day, I donned the business casual attire Janie had so meticulously selected, battled my way through rush-hour commutes, spent countless hours managing my pipeline, and suffered the endless tiresome meetings. No one else worked longer hours, and I'd accrued multiple expense reports full of costly client dinners and bar tabs. In many respects, I was a model account executive. Yet, while my colleagues closed deal after deal, I was subject to an interminable succession of losses.

In today's economy, where hyper-specialization is the key to success, a man in his mid-thirties has little chance to pursue new skills. I was convinced Janie would leave me when she learned I'd been fired. This was the fourth job I'd lost in as many years. My luck had been no better selling solar panels, commercial real estate, or fancy water machines. While all our friends scaled their respective corporate ladders and bought delightful homes, I had nothing to show for my decade in the city but a scroll of failure.

I didn't tell Janie I'd been fired again. Instead, I got up every morning, read the news with my grapefruit and espresso, donned my work attire, and headed cheerfully off to "work." But really, I was making art in Danny's studio. For years, I'd struggled with the idea I was nothing more than a dilettante. I hadn't jumped through any of the hoops required of a contemporary artist. I considered it undignified to pursue an MFA, and other than my friendship with Danny, I had no relations with anyone in the artistic community. This, too, frustrated Janie to no end.

"If you want to be an artist," she'd say, "you must do the things artists do!"

But her encouragement always rang false. Like all people who make a career of memorizing scientific facts and figures, Janie had little interest in the creative life. Her singular passion was to build a lucrative career that entrenched her as a respected member of the community, and afforded her a wardrobe of designer clothing and an apartment filled with luxury goods. And by her mid-thirties, but for one thing, her dreams had been fulfilled. Now she wanted to build a family.

"Let's make a baby!" she said one night, over our pad thai.

"Now may not be the best time," I said.

Janie couldn't understand. As a couple, she believed, we were doing better than most. She said that lately I'd seemed happier and more steadfast than ever. Somehow, I must have learned to find joy in corporate work, she reasoned. Her misconception, I knew, was due to my having ceased complaining about my job. She was right about my improved attitude. My days in the studio had proven a wonderful panacea. The real problem was, after months of unemployment, my resources were exhausted.

But just as things had turned for the worst, I tagged along with Danny to the racetrack. It took no more than a couple of races to see I had a psychic connection to the action. I needed only study how a horse approached the gate to know if it was a winner. After watching Danny burn through tens of thousands of dollars, I implored him to wager on a gelding named Bruno. The racing form told us Bruno had been running abysmally and was destined for the dog food factory. On this day, however, his stride was as smooth and easy as Denzel on the big screen, so I insisted. When Bruno won by six lengths, Danny gifted me twenty thousand dollars, money, I knew, that would sustain me for months.

This good fortune inspired me to tell Janie I'd quit my job to pursue art full-time. To prove my commitment, I brought her to the studio to view the series of sculptures I'd built out of lawn chairs and PVC piping. Her support evaporated on the spot. I was a derelict, Janie said, with no regard for her wishes or, most importantly, our future family.

Janie is nothing if not decisive, and she left that very night. I was so bereft that I went out drinking alone, telling myself Janie was merely trying to scare me. But the apartment when I got back was empty, as was my faith in the future. I had always sought new adventure, variety, novelty, but now all I wanted was the comfort and security I'd had with Janie.

To win her back, I spent my nights picking flowers that I lovingly placed at the door of her friend's apartment, where Janie was staying. Every day I'd hide behind a bush, waiting for her to leave for work, only to watch in dismay as she passed my offerings without so much as a glance. Finally, undeterred, I resorted to a most underhanded scheme: in a letter, I pleaded to let me give her a baby. I barred not a single hold. I detailed the sacrifices I'd make for our child, including learning the Chinese I'd someday teach him or her, knowing it to be a soft skill that could leverage tremendous advantages. But nothing I said would penetrate. Janie had made up her mind.

I started rifling through her things, letters from past boyfriends, photos from destinations foreign and remote, all these strange and arcane objects that now revealed the complete mystery Janie had been. I placed her underwear over my face, then masturbated on a stack of her cashmere sweaters. The next day, I woke in a pile on the bathroom floor, the underwear thick with vomit. I spent the morning writing a list of requests in my notebook, what I would pray for God to grant me. Why not resort to faith if it could be of some use?

That afternoon, I brought the sweaters to the dry cleaner. Seeing the stains, a little man with crooked teeth laughed so hard he knocked over a pile of folded clothes. A hunched woman whose face revealed decades of toil came out to click her tongue and pick at the stains with a dirty fingernail. Tiny flakes of milk-colored shame drifted to the floor. The sweaters, the man said, would be ready on Friday.

The day Janie came to pack her things, I worked in the studio on a painting of a dead boy in a coffin. At sunset, I shuffled home thinking Janie would be gone, but she hadn't finished. She handed me a check for her share of the rent for the remainder of the lease, and I presented her with a watercolor in which she was nude on a tropical beach, with the vague shape of an angel overhead.

LIKE ANYWHERE ELSE

by

AYLA ZURAW-FRIEDLAND

CHAPTER 1

You decide to bring bread to Mother.

When you open your eyes on the day of the referendum, you are thinking of bananas, of lemon. On the news the anchor speaks with the same breathlessness of the past month. The future of the city hangs in the balance. You crack two eggs into a bowl.

The story shifts to updates about the boy. He is awake but still does not speak. He only points to God. You think "allegedly" as you chase a sliver of shell through the egg whites with your fingertip.

Banana bread is really more like cake. There is no yeast, nothing living to it.

You have bowls of wet and dry ingredients and no time to wait for anything to rise. The anchor with her wardrobe of satin white chemises confirms this—the polls are open now and will close at 7pm tonight. You study her face. Rumor has it she was sent here to Saudade after killing her child during a night terror attack because she thought he was an intruder. You fold the flour into the banana mash that looks like baby food. Her foundation crinkles beneath her eyes like a plaster wall. For all the time you've spent watching the news, watching her, you've never been able to decide if you think the rumor is true or whether it would matter if it was. You watch as bits of setting powder float down to her blazer.

You pat the remaining residue of banana paste beneath your own eyes. It is something between war paint and retinol. Whatever she did doesn't matter. The referendum is today. You will bring Mother the loaf. You will ask why she stopped talking to you, if there's anything you can do to help. You will vote yes.

The banana bread is in the oven. You skipped the walnuts. For all of the attention you have paid to Mother—her moods, her habits—you do not know for sure whether she is allergic to nuts. This troubles you. It reminds you that she is not yours alone. Despite the practiced informality of her title, she is really only the mayor's mother. Mayor mother. You set to making a glaze. It's just sugar and water, but it makes everything feel more celebratory.

Before your roommate Cora left that morning, she asked how you planned to vote. Usually Cora looked immaculate, but today her skin was dull, eyes hooded by sleeplessness. You didn't hear her come home the night before even though you'd dozed off in front of the TV. For a moment you were offended. It didn't seem there was really any other choice.
"I'm voting yes," you said, resting the edge of your lip on the round of your coffee mug, its contents gone cold for the second time.

Cora nodded at you, approving. Something flared within you, an irritation you had come to associate with Cora over the months you'd lived together. It felt as though she were testing you, judging. You were both here in this city for people with secrets. Was that not proof enough that you were the same?

"See you there," she said. Then, before you could turn the question back to her, she was putting in her headphones and adjusting the volume to something you could hear across the room. And gone.

In truth, you like Cora, you think. She has been kind to you, if distant, especially when you first arrived in Saudade. When you crouched on the floor of the bathroom on those nights anxiety and homesickness and guilt turned you inside out until all you could do was spit long strings of saliva into the toilet, she rubbed your back in slow, generous circles. "No one wants to be the unlucky one."

Now you prefer not to wonder what switched in her when she pulled away. She never told you what she did to end up here, and you knew better than to ask who she had taken from herself or others. Or perhaps you were too squeamish to push.

"It's a sad, long story. I'll tell you when you're feeling better," she'd dodged. You let her.

In truth you weren't sure if you felt better, or if you were growing numb to the memory of the sunlight through the windshield, of blood spreading to fill the veins of cracked asphalt. Perhaps the repetition of telling had wrung out the color, the potency, until it was just another story.

The clock on the stove is ten minutes ahead or behind. You can never remember which. You could swear it switches back and forth. In any case, you will leave for Mother's by noon.

Take the bus across the city.

They said Saudade would keep you safe. You would find solace and kinship with others who had been through this. A city of people who had killed others entirely by accident. Of doctors, who in their 32nd hour on their feet, had ordered a patient a fatal dose of morphine, of amateur chefs gathering deathcap mushrooms mistaken for puffballs for the quiche, of teenage boys pushing one another into the shallow ends of pools. You gnawed at the raw, metallic flesh of your lip as you listened to the counselor. It sounded too good to be true. You had searched for others like you in online chatrooms, in the eyes of strangers, on the streets of your hometown and found nothing. But here they all were, thriving, or at least learning to cope, away from the prying of everyone who knew without knowing, who had seen you sobbing outside of the police station begging them to take you day after day, to excise the weight of knowing: it was you, it was you, it was you.

*

It is 12:15 by the time you make it to the bus. You didn't leave enough time for the loaf to cool in your calculus of the day. With one eye on the clock you had fanned it with a pot lid. You placed it in the freezer, hoping that the time it took you to wash the mixing bowls and wipe the counters again would be enough. The icing liquified on contact anyways and you told yourself it wasn't so bad, even as the surface crumbed and broke beneath the butter knife you used to spread it.

Now the loaf tin is mockingly warm against your torso. You try not to watch the icing congeal like bits of bacon fat. It'll at least taste good, homemade. It'll be the thought that counts.

You read a pamphlet taped to the glass of the stop. It is pinned open like a moth on display. Whoever wrote it spelled refugee with two fs and thought it was in Saudade's best interest to be "thoughtful" about who they granted entry to the city. The chipper automated voice of the bus tracker assures you and the other passengers that a bus is three minutes away for the fourth time in nearly twenty minutes. No buses arrive.

Months earlier you had stood at the same stop when you met Mother for the first time.

"Where are you going?" She had placed a feather-light hand on your shoulder, barely disturbing the fabric of your jacket.

"Town hall," you told the tiny woman who only came up to your chin. "But I think I might be going the wrong way."

She was not yet Mother to you. You had arrived two weeks beforeand that was your first time out of the apartment provided to you by the city, first time you had showered and dressed well enough to explore. You had told yourself you needed time to adjust, and now your caseworker had determined it was time for you to start the job you had been assigned to with the city's historical society—a good use, you think, of your atrophying museum studies degree. Mother was not Mother until a few days later when you sat at the welcome desk waiting for someone to visit the museum, which was really just a single room waiting for history to be made. You recognized her from the bus and thanked her for helping you read the schedule.

She nodded and gave the tight but somehow not quite pained smile you now recognized as her default when dealing with strangers. It was poise with caution, a biting back of warmth.

"I'm the mayor's mother," she said, extending a surprisingly strong, dry hand. "But everyone here calls me Mother." You asked if she needed anything, if she wanted to come in. You could already feel yourself being drawn to her. You always had a knack for seeking out more mothers—in teachers, in bosses, in your girlfriends and classmates.

Mother demurred. She was on her way to meet her actual daughter for lunch in her office down the hall. She just wanted to see how you were settling in.

"You'll be okay," she said, giving something like a wink. When she was gone, you replayed that exchange over and over. Had she really paused as if to say something else? Or was it just her pressing her lips together to smooth out unseen lumps in her chapstick? It wasn't so much the loneliness of being in Saudade that got to you. It was of course difficult being away from the people you knew, your collection of mothers left behind when you ran from the housefire of your life after the accident. It was the feeling of being the least enlightened. Everyone around you seemed so at peace with themselves, so accepting of what they couldn't change. You had tried. You were trying to read the book that all residents were given when they arrived. The advice for guided meditation bounced off your brain, glossy like the pages of your Drivers Permit manual from another life.

You and Mother developed something verging on a friendship. Small exchanges at the desk on her way to weekly lunches.

More frequent visits, sitting and knitting while you filed paperwork. And then the extra loaves of sourdough she left at your desk. The rest of the city only got them in her weekly deliveries, but you felt your jawline sharpen with the effort of the constant chewing. You lived on that bread.

Now you wait. You've been waiting for thirty minutes for this bus, and three weeks for any word from Mother after she very suddenly stopped coming to the museum. Today you will confront her. Today perhaps the headaches and dreams will subside when you've proven that she is okay. You are not known for speaking up, for arriving uninvited. But what use were those rules? They hadn't saved you in your old life. Maybe now you could become the kind of person people smiled at, who could just drop by with a loaf of banana bread and some gossip. Maybe you could become lovable. Maybe you could have photos of other people on your phone instead of just yourself proving to yourself that you exist.

You study the faces of other passengers. It is hard to tell whether the furrowing of brows is for the missing bus or the weight of where the bus will take them. You play a game and try to guess how each of them will vote. Some of them wear buttons which takes some of the fun out of it—"Vote No to Foes", "Yes to all". But the rest are blank slates. They all tap their fingers against the handles of folded umbrellas. They all heave sighs when the bus tracker voice pipes up again. You all wait to see what is coming.

You will arrive at Mother's, loaf in hand. You will ask where she has been—careful not to whine, to accuse.
And there is still the matter of the headaches. Of the notes

stuck to the bottom of the bread delivered to your apartment in the regular deliveries, which, despite Mother's disappearance, continued like clockwork.

You try not to think of the notes. How they alternate between vitriol (*You are disgusting how can you keep living and eating and shitting and knowing about the rain when you've had a man crushed beneath your tires?*) and apology (*I know it was an accident. I can hardly imagine. Wendell's death gave me my life back.*) They are inside of you, anyways. Each crumpled and chewed to pulp, washed down with your coffee. You imagine the ratio of blood to ink in your veins tilting ounce by ounce.

The letters technically started before Mother stopped coming to the town hall. But had she not started acting strangely before? Had you not spent evenings troubling over the moment of the shift in her demeanor? Beating yourself over the head with your own want as punishment for not noticing the exact second Mother ceased to be the person you needed her to be? For making it about yourself once again? There must have been something before she started wearing the gloves, the masks, the enormous sunglasses she called her bug eyes? Had you even asked?

You had gone to the mayor's office to inquire. There was no reason to deliver the weekly museum log (blank, as usual) by hand. As you stood over the mayor's desk waiting for her to notice your shadow when she looked up from whatever she was writing, you counted the greys sprouting from her scalp.

"Has Mother been to visit?" she asked you without meeting your eyes, not pausing in her work. The mayor had always reminded you of an automaton—the staccato of her movements, how her neck moved as though it was swiveling on ball bearings rather than muscle and bone.

"I came here to ask you the same thing," you told her. You stepped closer. The mayor still didn't look up. But you could see what she's been writing. A page full of the same phrase: It's like anywhere else.

Until the referendum, until the boy's disappearance and return that started it all, until the notes and the searing pain of a headache that made your ears ring, you had felt safe in Saudade. That was the point. Being here removed any possibility of revenge enacted by the friends or lovers or family of the dead. It took you away from those who knew what you'd done and had no idea how to treat you as a result. You had come to, if not love, at least gratefully accept the hitherto unheard of benefits of group therapy designed for people like you and your new neighbors. The relief of not explaining yourself had cured your back pain, your stutter, your skittishness being around cars. Saudade was built with all of you in mind. The corners of your world were dulled down until nothing could be wielded. There was never sun in your eyes. Everyone had a job, but only insofar as they all contributed to the functioning of the city in return for housing, for a stipend, for medicine and produce taken freely from the shelves of pharmacies and grocery stores. It was everything those on the outside wanted, and what a strange irony to have killed to get it.

Your favorite thing about Saudade is the first Thursday of every month. The city hosts a movie night, projecting a family

-friendly film on the white stucco of city hall. It isn't the fact of the movie you love—though your heart swells at the sight of residents sprawled on blankets across the green—heads on laps, elbows bent to support their weight. The children from the House of Youth sit at the front, small sticky hands crushing plastic dixie cups of popcorn. Your favorite part is the short history of Refuge Cities that plays before the movie starts. It's arguably propaganda, but you don't care. You could recite the voiceover explanation of the first six cities—God's desire for safety, the shepherd and shepherdess, the abyss and the village idiot—from memory.

You are always impatient for one image. At the end there is one of God—or at least the wide flat palm blocking their face from the camera. Their hair is wild, frizzing out of braids in a crown. Through the spaces between their fingers, you can see their mouth has been captured in the split second between a scowl intended to ruin the fun and the photo of whoever has the camera, and the surprise of a laugh coaxed out by the same person. You know they are powerful and there's something calculated about using a photograph so blatantly candid. It feels calculated, like a class clown or edgelord doing something expectedly unexpected for a yearbook photo. It's a tuxedo t-shirt at prom. It's bunny ears or a middle finger. It's blinking.

When you see this photo, you feel a leap of recognition in the faded red t-shirt, the can of energy drink next to the keyboard. Identifying with a god is dangerous – that's why it's a complex. But the humanity of blocking the flash of a point-and-shoot camera, the way it erases the creases of the palm into noth-ing—no lifeline, no heartline or freckles—the fact that there are photos like this in albums and hard drives and flea markets everywhere, that's what made you feel safest.

The bus comes, finally, it noses to the stop and the crowd tries to pack itself into the already full vehicle. If anyone can hear the harried driver promising there is another bus just behind him, just a minute away, they don't show it.

"There's a protest down by the House of Youth," someone says. "They wouldn't move."

The impossible clown car physics of public transit goes into effect. Ordinarily people would be tripping over themselves to be the patient ones who waited for the next bus. But not to-day. Today there is a pull of stiff efficiency, of time unwilling to bend. The weeks of uncertainty have crescendoed to this.

The loaf is balanced in the crook of one arm like a baby and you use your other hand to catch one of the straps hang-ing from the bar above you. But you have something else to attend to first. It is not that you do not care about the fate of the city, or that you aren't also checking for news of the boy —whether he has woken, whether the doctors think he can or will ever speak again. It is that, regardless of any outcome, you cannot imagine Saudade continuing to exist without Mother. You are not sure if it is something about you or about her that keeps here. When you try to think of things you know about Mother that are not things she has given you—solace, sourdough, softness—you draw a blank. It took every ounce of self-control not to ask why you were the recipient of the extra loaf of bread, why she chose you. And now that was spent. You needed to know why she had come for you, and now why she had left.

The bus creaks forward, protesting against your collective weight. All is quiet. Even children on their parents' laps are respectful of this gravitas, despite the obvious absurdity of grown men pressed nose to nose with strangers and pretending not to be. You would laugh, but your voice would be the only sound.

The focus in Saudade was not on what any of you had done to qualify as citizens. But everyone seemed to know. Everyone kept their own ranking of where they felt they stood as compared to their neighbors in terms of severity of situation. Everyone would lie if anyone asked what it was.

*

You knew, of course, what you did.

A car accident, nothing exciting.

It was in the newspaper, but only because Saturdays in small towns are news deserts. You were on the front page. Not you, actually, your car. They did not print your name. Only the name of the dead: Wendell Derry. He was a weekend warrior training for a 10k to raise money for pancreatic cancer. He was married. He had worked for the law offices of Barrett and Liu as an attorney for twenty years without making partner, and then as a part-time law librarian when he retired eight years ago. He was survived by his wife and stepdaughter and father and sister. His college fraternity helped plan the funeral. In lieu of flowers, donations to the fund for Bernie's chemo. It's what Wendell would have wanted.

You told Mother all of this the first time you met for lunch. It was sunny. Mother busied her hands with a tangle of crochet and yarn that crowned from her purse. She listened, only interrupting to ask if the sun was in your eyes then, and to ask the server for more hot water for her tea.

"How did it feel?" she asked once you had blown your nose into every available napkin at the table.

You started to tell her about the guilt, about the dreams, about how you felt your atoms slip and shed until suddenly, you were here.

"No," she stops you. "How did it feel?"

And then you realized she was asking an entirely different question. One you had never been directly asked. One no one wanted to reveal they craved the answer to. You watched her hands. They seem to move across the yarn of their own accord. You took a deep breath, three stitches long, as you willed the courage to look at her face when you told her.

"Like nothing. Like an animal."

She nodded in approval. Eyes distant but perhaps only because she had taken off her glasses. It was part of the story you'd never told. You half expected to be whisked away for this confession, for admitting you perhaps lacked the humanity or intuition to have felt, somehow, the soul of a body depart the way that everyone else talked about. Instead, you had felt the impact, slammed the brakes, more out of reflex than concern, and pulled over to the shoulder. You didn't even put the hazard lights on when you got out of the car to assess the damage.

Now you adjust the loaf tin, still warm. It's a paltry gift, you think. It doesn't match all that Mother gave you. But it's what you have.

*

There was the story of Saudade everyone knew. Everyone knew it was the seventh city, the newest, the experiment. Despite it being completely random that they were the ones to end up here, there was a sense of pride in it. It was God's special project; that must mean they were special. But it was unclear how the city had come to this—a moment of reckoning they were meant to be insulated from.

You disembark a stop earlier than everyone else, elbowing the other passengers until they shuffle to let you through. It's raining now as you walk the half block to the sage-shuttered house where Mother lives. The drizzle feels appropriate. You wonder, for the umpteenth or the first time, if the weather in Saudade can be felt over the border. Or, if the refugees just on the other side are watching all of you as though you are in a snow globe just out of reach. You give a cautious wave to the treeline. You don't know if it's meant as an acknowledgment that could save you later if they remember you waved, or if you really mean it. Like everything, perhaps it is both.

Things weren't always like this. You didn't always know about the refuge cities or acts of God or how a body compresses when it is crushed. You say this as a mantra but you can't remember for sure what came before.

TIME FOR A CHOCOLATE

by

REBECCA PYLE

CHAPTER ONE:
A LAND ROVER

Now Gavin was a rich man, an international chocolatier. He drove a Land Rover, or the Land Rover drove him, sending him roving to the land of roving. Once he lived in London; now he lived in the valleys of the exhausted young man, Oxford, a different land where people like him rested after the dramas of school attendance and jail sentence completion and inheriting money from fathers, whoever or wherever each might be, were complete. For him there had only been a few women and oddly none were dark-haired, as he was; all were blonde with hair so much the same shade of very dull blonde some said his own mother must be blonde the same way—he must be trying to replace her with another blonde just like her. This drew a laugh from him only his closest friends could understand. She had not even left a photograph.

Yet now he might find her. If you were adopted and rich, ah, you were a plum in the pudding. The adoption agency, The Dish Ran Away with the Spoon, was located in Shepherd's Bush in West London, across from a series of driving schools run by aging boys from Kuala Lumpur who had cousins who ran budding footwear stores. The staff at The Dish Ran Away with the Spoon looked with interest at the shiny black car parked out front with its hood symbol that looked like a steadied steering wheel or star. They looked with interest at his Burberry plaid scarf, at his heavy silver ring not on his wedding-band hand,

and his burgundy leather boots. They did not, as he expected they would not, ask him about any criminal record. They noticed with interest that he was related to the author James Arthur who had written science fiction, then somehow turned it to plays, one of which had even had a short run in the West End. They nodded a lot about this; then they stopped nodding, and their eyes cleared.

She's here, they said.

You don't mean here, he said.

No, we don't mean here, they said. We mean in this country.

In England? he said. He was already thinking of how far he would have to drive his Land Rover.

We'll take you there, they said. Two of them were talking, the gentle washed-out old man who did not wear a suit but instead a brown mohairy cardigan sweater, and the tricked-up young lady attendant, twenty-two possibly and the kind of young woman who would once have been a secretary before modern answering machines. She agreed with everything the older man said, even his opinion that it was best if children were placed in 'more successful' homes. He had used that phrase three times in the past few minutes after Gavin appeared.
And why do that? said Gavin.

You'll see, and it would be best if you see, rather than we describe, the older man said. His eyes were following Gavin, waiting for his yes. He reminded Gavin of who his adoptive father might have been if he had not had his successes: nothing but a wish to facilitate, to help, if a salary was involved. But you could tell the adoption agency man, whose name was Mr. Reeves, also had a soul: when tea was brought in by the young assistant, he took the tray from her with an eaglish swoop that brought a smile to her cosmeticized face and he sent her off to an early lunch.

The better, Mr. Reeves said, to explain things to you.

Gavin's face enrolled in worry.

Don't worry that way, Mr. Reeves said. Every child wants to know his story. Do you know the Fairfield Home?

It sounded a little like the dry house Gavin had been sent to after his release from prison (which his father had successfully orchestrated), the miserable dry house where they were testing everyone to see if they'd go crazy with their troubling provoking habits again, invading other people's lives with their determined drug or sex or gun joys. Their every word was written down and their beds had limp unraveling hems, but there was excellent dinner, a little card that sent them to the fish and chips shop each night and entitled them to a full pound of fish and chips on greased newsprint, which made Gavin think of the many-folded newspapers that formed make-believe hats when he was a child. Those paper-hat years were the years his father had first filled him and his older brother in on the reasons neither of them had that perfect fairy called a mother.

Fairfield Home, Gavin said. Sounds very pretty.

Oh, it's not, said Mr. Reeves, cheerfully. He set down his tea-cup. But it's alright, it really is, and if you want I'll call them.

Gavin nodded.

The Fairfield Home was a dignified, signified place. Its great trees rose up with their arching branches as if to make you look below to the grove where a stone path cut through the neat lawn to the portico. It was a sprawl of a walk, but not a walk you wanted to walk on long, as the doors ahead filled you with some worry. What could have been the gracious doors of a country home were now institutional doors with militantly gleaming glass, an expanse wide enough to permit even side-by-side wheelchairs enough room to make it through one of the doors without parting.

Tell me now, Gavin wanted to say, is something terribly wrong with my mother? But he was as if at the edge of a chocolate box, fearing offending the person who was offering him his choice of sweets. He dreaded the dead-tasting little peanut turtles, the cheap over-sweet peppermint creams with their thin pours of chocolate on top, the beetle-like ovals of coconut creams with their desperate need to sugarify coconut, pulverized and vatted in some hellish corn-syrupy doom. The cardboard box with its fresh paper wrapping would be in the landfill with last week's sterilized milk cartons and rolls from paper towels. But now its bright it-cost-some-money-for-this-special-occasion edge was telling him Time for a Chocolate.

He was not in France, where a man wearing four different shades of green with sleepy eyes might be handing him a few inches of rosemary he had pulled from a shrub by the door, and also, in the same arm gesture, might be showing him a pot of melted butter-dredged chocolate, holding its silvery handles, indicating rosemary dipped in that chocolate, surprise, really was not bad. He was not with his old travel mate, Baj, who must be now at this time ignoring the man in four shades of green in France and instead might be looking deep into an empty cement wine vat under a wooden canopy two dozen steps beyond the rosemary-chocolatier, wondering where the wine business had gone, and about to ask the chocolatier if the vats could be converted back for the makings of any kind of chocolate, instead of wine. All would sell well with the right labels.

He was at the Fairfield Home, where almost everyone employed there worked for the simple fact of salary. There were few affectations.

We're going to see your mother, Mr. Reeves said. We've cleared it with her.

And the home? Gavin said.

No need for that, Mr. Reeves said. This is her matter. Not theirs. She made clear to me that she is not ready to see... you... in her home. Not yet.

Oh, thank all the gods—she's not a resident here, Gavin said.

Not a resident, said Mr. Reeves, though I think it would have been nicer meeting, say, at a restaurant. But we've had clients who say they can forget all about eating when they meet their parent for the first time. They are struck by how difficult it is sitting across from someone at a table and wondering how many meals this person ate without them.

I see, said Gavin. Awful thought.

Room 203, Mr. Reeves said. His brown cardigan was blending very nicely with the vanilla walls of Fairfield Home. He looked like Gavin's uncle or possibly the son of someone trundling on wheels through the crème-colored halls, finally now taking time out to visit the entrapped misery of the residents here in the hopes that his virtue would make him humbler and happier in his life. People passed him in wheelchairs with an expression on their faces that said they realized thusly that someone among them might be the dispenser of blessings, rather than something withheld. Gavin could see them brightening. They looked at Gavin; he had brightened them. But how could his mother be here and yet have a home too? Short-term problem? As he, Gavin, had obviously been? He defined the smell of the place as wintergreen mixed with white narcissus and let himself fall behind Mr. Reeves. The way Mr. Reeves was walking showed his certainty that this young man in his late thirties, present here, was definitely good news. For anyone.

The teacher, Mr. Reeves said, pointing.

She was exceptionally tall, and her clothes were exceptionally strange. A white fake-fur boa was looped once-and-a-half around her neck; she had red tiered earrings hanging down like dollhouse bordello chandeliers. Her neck was wrinkled and she wore a deep boat-neck aqua leotard. The skirt she wore was known as a broomstick skirt, the kind that if it wrinkled you were supposed to smooth out the fabric by wrapping it around a broom. The skirt was a gauzy printed material with a puzzling design. She wore black ballet flats, the kind schoolgirls wore during dance classes to avoid the expense, bother, and pain of pointe shoes with their wooden blocks in the toes and the bloodstains inside them after all the bending, flexing, and posing with crumpled toes on those blocks; the skin on the top of her feet had begun to wrinkle and collect freckles. Her arms were raised in a half-circle above her head.

Lift, she said. Lift.

In front of her, the geriatrics and the physically troubled and tormented lifted their arms, or at least tried to lift them with a pained look that suggested they had been told to attend class.

But Gavin had not been told; he had asked her if he could come.

She did not stop when she saw Gavin come into the room. She kept going. Perhaps she had not really wanted to see him. He could imagine Mr. Reeves stressing how much time and money Gavin had spent driving all the way here, that nothing very distressing could go on in her place of work. It would be a pleasant, short visit. This young man wouldn't say anything inappropriate. He would keep it light. Polite. He would just say hello and talk with her after class.

Stop now, said Gavin. It's me.

She raised her very old eyes to him that had once been so full of life.

THE MOTH FOR THE STAR

by

JAMES REICH

CHAPTER 1

Five years later, Charles Varnas would recall the white linen against his shin, the shifting blade of his trousers, one knee folded across the other. How different was that sharp angle of flax in the Cairo breeze from the geometry of the shaving razor, dripping blood in his right hand? The razor was like an architect's tool, something an astrologer might employ, an astronomer's quadrant. All the clean angles of a murder— How agreeable it was to discover that as he reclined against the warm dune, he might align the cool material of his pant leg with the chrome yellow slant of the pyramids cutting the cloudless sky. He was, quite simply, a dark-haired man in a pale suit who had been on a long voyage. Across the mercury of that distance, he would remember this. They had struggled, he and the dead one beside him—the Adversary—cloven red as a sacrificial animal, its skin stiffening. The pulsing blood had suggested the bloom of amaranth. Charles Varnas reposed on that slope of sand, attentive to the heat of his breath, the approach of black, the welcome he gave his strange tears, and the infinite melancholy that would reach for him from the stars like a mob of brilliant spiders—

All of this returned to him again in the gasoline air of Lexington Avenue, at noon on the first Monday of September 1930, when a stray sheet of newsprint wrapped around his ankle. Like an awkward bird, Charles Varnas lifted his foot and plucked at the paper now fluttering against his shin, extending the tan briefcase that held his folding Smith Corona as a counterbalance at the edge of the sidewalk. He studied the page. It was from yesterday's Times. That drab Sunday had been witness to the sallow scrawl of breadlines, rain falling on long coats and declining furs boned with hunger. As he examined the newspaper sheet, between a story on air racing in Chicago, and what could be made of the laconic minutes saved by riding the trolley through the new system of traffic signals, something grandiose in the stray columns of type appealed to him. It insinuated like a rumor, whispering through his flesh as he stared at the headline: HOPES OF IMMORTALITY. With his briefcase pressed between his elbow and ribs, Varnas folded the newspaper page into a rectangular wad, slipping it into the breast pocket of his herringbone sports coat behind his leather notebook and his pen. Later, he would cut out the columns of the report that attracted him. For now, Varnas had some intuition to protect this omen that had come to push him back into his past. Lexington Avenue dissolved—

He was there again, with the pyramids under the desert twilight, the dune darkening with gore. He felt the slick oily coating of anise and fennel in his mouth as he watched the Pernod bottle rolling soundlessly away across the sand. He sensed the promise of evening, of a rendezvous when it was over. And there was the terrible corpse, faceless, indistinct under the greasy muslin of forgetting, witnessed through the narrowing aperture of his sorrow, all the hieroglyphs of violence. It had been Charles Varnas' twenty-fifth birthday, and his second visit to Egypt. Now, he was a murderer. Yet, he could not recall his victim in any detail, only the presence of a profound danger ebbing into the desert, to be borne away like someone drowning in the undulating sand. The true nature of the Adversary seemed to drift from his consciousness, and if he sought it with any aggressive attention, it merely evaded him more determinedly. It was as though some glamor of amnesia protected him, so that he could never give himself away. Who could confess what he did not recall? In a matter of hours, he would lose any sense of guilt at the act. It was necessary, after all, was it not? As he searched himself, it was, perhaps, the first moment of absolute confidence he had experienced. At last, he got to his feet. Unfamiliar constellations measured Varnas in their cool threads as he made his exit. The corpse would clot and sink, drawn under to vanish in those golden tenements of time.

Dipping his shaving razor into the silent surface of the desert, Varnas wiped the paste of blood and dust from the steel with his index finger and repeated this gesture until it was clean. In the future, he would be able to see his motions like a religious ritual, but now it felt like a childish preoccupation to make one thing perfect. He rubbed his finger and thumb together until the evidence vanished from the blade into his pores or was stripped and rolled into sticky pills against his skin. He had done the same with his seaweed colored mucous in childhood. Varnas' childhood had been constellated with cruelty, with figures set to hurt him, a sense of loss, and of being turned against what he loved.

He took out his handkerchief. There was time to polish the razor once more before closing and pocketing it. In the rising wind, he discarded the cloth, and lit a cigarette behind his cupped hand. He recalled walking carelessly back toward the suburbs of the city, sensing his shallow wake of footfalls being erased, the dunes enwrapping the body far behind him, sifting the blood down, lowering the heavy flesh, the bright bones, and its mask of disbelief into the slow waves of the desert. Infinitely, it would turn and fall into its vanishing.

It had seemed to Varnas that he walked for hours, one long howling street through Giza where the late trams rattled, the billboards peeled, and bare lightbulbs whined. This was the street he had first seen as a boy in 1912, with his father and mother. He removed his jacket, holding it in the crook of his arm like a matador's cape. The night air was cold against the Rorschach image at the division of his spine, his shirt becoming transparent, revealing something like a flesh-colored moth of sweat. Red embers and sweet cigarette smoke signaled the approach of scattered men, skimming him, quick as phantom children, their voices urgent and indecipherable. He was not afraid of them, as he might have been before, walking instead with a new killer's insouciance. A Suez Company oil drum burned between a crowd of brittle men in a side street. Sparks coiled upward into the darkness, then fell back. Down the street, a soldier slept in a raffia chair. In the moonlight, two others leaned against a blanketed camel, whispering over their revolvers in the animal's acrid shadow, nostalgic for the fighting of 1919. Varnas stepped between warm turrets of dung. He experienced a cool sense of being dispossessed. For now, those particular ghosts that harrowed him from abroad, from Oxford, Manchester, Niagara Falls, and the blear past of his Eastern European ancestors, they all declined from him, letting him almost alone. The ghosts were silent, confused by his determination, his dignity in victory.

Crossing the English Bridge and the Kobri El Gezira with its great bronze lions over the blackening Nile, he pulled his hip flask from his pocket and finished the gin he had saved for the return. Something was ascendent in him, vivid as a new star. Leaning on his elbows at the balustrade, he was midway across the bridge span. Varnas retrieved the razor from his other pocket, weighing it in his palm. The river was slow beneath him, assumed by the moon. It amused him that he could never look down from a vantage like this bridge or a tall building without imagining how it would be to jump. In the roadway at his back, a tubercular police motorcycle rasped, bearing its rider westward. He was alone. Without another thought, without opening it again, he let the razor fall into the Nile. Then, he slicked his black hair back from his eyes and walked on. It was late when he reached Ezbekiya where the white palm trunks stood like the pillars of a mausoleum. The killing was far behind him. It was all so distant that when he reached Khaled's Place with its exhausted cabaret, bad drinks, and impenetrable coffee, he could not recall why he had gone out that day—

In Manhattan now, blond-haired Charles Varnas walked briskly toward the Chrysler Building and his luncheon appointment. He had become quite used to the peroxide. It concealed his true nature, he thought, whatever that was. He did not care if, at times, the stark roots showed at his scalp. That had become his way of expressing something about which he was otherwise inarticulate. The sun came clutching and clawing between the tall buildings, as though it might snatch the weakest flesh off the street. Walking pleased him. Passing beneath the awnings and flags of the new Bloomingdale's, his slim form had flashed in the glass and the gloss of its facade. Those who might have encountered Varnas on that day at the beginning of September 1930 would have been struck by his flinty good looks, the blue eyes that squinted in his adopted American concentration always upon the future —eclipsing even his natural English disposition toward the past—the white crow's feet revealed by the flickering sunlight, that slight but perpetual tension in the jaw, and the grit of his teeth that came from too many escaped ideas, always just out of reach. Perhaps it was the pressure of keeping the past at bay. For, that day, the past interrupted, manipulated, and haunted his image of himself. Putting a finger to the thin scar beside his right eye, he wished he could have a drink, and wondered if he regretted coming home. Alcohol was still difficult to find.

At least, he thought, the metallic ministry of the Chrysler was some consolation. The most beautiful building in the world, it had been—fleetingly—the tallest. He strode under the entrance, an open sarcophagus of jet and aluminum, into the tobacco vault of the lobby. To Varnas, it suggested eternity, as though the great skyscraper had fused the future to the past in dreaming angles of marble, and gnostic light in golden pillars. The effect presented a space so strange that alchemists and aviators might repair in its elevators, their tomb doors inlaid with fanning papyrus leaves. Varnas did not care for Chrysler's automobiles, but the trappings of the man's wealth in this tower were luminous and magnificent, like the mad amber crypt of some new Akhenaton. When Varnas was a child, he had put a coin in his mouth and tasted the bitter blood taste of money. Now, like the shadow of a bird, pleasure passed over his features as he anticipated his ascent to the 66th floor and the Cloud Club.

Inside the elevator, he set down his briefcase and removed the folded page of newspaper from his breast pocket. He registered the narrow bite of sorrow that came as his fingers traced the ink. It reminded him of holding nettles as a boy. It was strange how much of his childhood interrupted him, of late. As much as he tried to live in the present, and to fix his version of the future in his mind, unpleasant recollections pressed upon him. He had tried to address his obsessive thoughts. Yes, he would say to himself, you have had that thought before. There is nothing to be gained by repeating it.

The news column that now compelled him like a curse concerned a Harvard lecture by a man named Robert Falconer, President of the University of Toronto. This man Falconer had declaimed on "The Idea of Immortality and Western Civilization." As the elevator rose, Varnas read how Falconer had spoken of the years before the War, and of the decline of the Christian spirit, such as it was, or whatever that was. Varnas was not a Christian. He was not certain what he was.

In the absence of any other image of Falconer, Varnas imagined him as a limpid, tortured Jesuit type. He superimposed a shovel-jawed photograph he had seen of the poet Gerard Manley Hopkins—*dapple-dawn-drawn Falcon, in his riding / Of the rolling level underneath him steady air*—in all the places where Falconer's name appeared. The poet Hopkins occupied one of the constellations of Varnas' being: the leather-bound notebook that Varnas kept at his breast contained pencil and ink transcriptions of Hopkins' poems. The handwriting was not Varnas' own, but from someone he had known. Despite the barbed wire of the script and the bad memories, the poems transcended, somehow. He kept it deliberately close to his heart. There was space after the copies of Hopkins' poems for including his own on several blank pages. Despite himself, Varnas had not written a poem in many years. Perhaps he was doing Falconer a disservice with his imaginary physical comparison to Hopkins. Nevertheless, he thought, didn't all men cut the world to the limits of their own cloth? It did not hurt too much to admit that one's imagination was limited.

Images of the desert pulled at him. Perhaps keeping the poems was a mistake. Did they conspire with this stray newsprint that caught him in the street? Varnas winced, stiffened his legs, and studied the article. The Times recorded something of Falconer's lecture to his audience. Varnas read, "There were no clouds upon the hills, no mystery. In that atmosphere, men's faces lost their softer tones and their eyes grew keen. Material success affected them almost to elation. It was but a step from this into the sheer paganism that was frankly permitted to reign in the great cities of Western civilization."

Varnas wondered if this Falconer had lost money in the stock market. Hanging in the melancholy amber light of the elevator and ascending rapidly skyward as if in a dream of his own death, Varnas could only marvel at the smooth surfaces of this "sheer paganism," the gentle fingerprint on the golden console that selected the floors, and the ghosts of nicotine and pomade. Briefly, he imagined the elevator falling in its shaft. It must have felt that way last year if one had money of one's own. Varnas did not.

He was hungry, yet the hunger was pleasant evidence of being alive. It put him in touch with other people. Even the slight motion sickness he felt was reassuring. According to the newspaper article, Falconer had gone on to say that with all the sacrifices of the species to spirit and reason, it could only be reasonable that—even if the physical universe might not provide—some providential realm must surely exist for the more tender and faithful disciples of progress. He was talking about an everlasting afterlife, eternity in paradise. Would that logic—that life was simply so unbearable that there must be a Heaven—appeal to the breadlines? Had men considered this as gas drifted across the bloody trenches? It struck Varnas as naive. Immortality, he thought, was more arduous than that. Did immortality not contain its own hungers, its own agonies, sudden or eternal? Did not the hunger for being have its limits? Had not his own face come to appear lean and vicious, betraying the shortening rope of his existence and his desire for more? There were many reasons why a face might lose its softness, he thought, and not all of them material.

Varnas folded the paper and returned it to his breast pocket, fitting it carefully behind his notebook and pen. In time, he would write something new in the notebook. He might yet return to the talons and thorns of poetry—that which he had loved first and lost—and to the vision of himself like meat swung on a thread that he had hungered after. But, for the present, it contained only a pencil drawing he had made of something like an awkward heron at the place where the copies of Hopkins' poems left off, its wings in gray lead spread on the creme paper, its beak too long. There was nothing after. He had drawn it weeks ago, and now it waited at his breast with a breathing inevitability. These things, he thought, collaborated. Time murmured obscenities.

Chapter 2

From the elevator, Varnas strode to the upholstered doors that opened to the Cloud Club. Its oak-paneled roar poured like dirty gravel upon a coffin. Varnas scanned the room. Even through the obscurity of cigar smoke, the absence of women struck him immediately and unpleasantly. It always did. The men there talked of little that was not technical or bureaucratic. Easing through knots of dull conversation, he approached the crowded staircase. Men were discussing their businesses there, also. It struck him as being in bad taste, and tedious, but he was not certain what they should be talking about. The discovery of a new planet, perhaps. He had been thinking about it, intermittently, for months. Did it sustain life, this new and distant globe? What about the new DeMille, *Madam Satan*, with its orgy of costume parties on a doomed Zeppelin? What about life and death, fear versus courage, good versus evil, philosophy, sport, astrology, or speculations over anything but business? They should let women in, Varnas thought. Gripping the brass banister, experiencing himself sharply as an intruder, he ascended. Furtively, he scanned the charcoal and ivory murals of mechanics on the walls of bright carmine. At last, he came to the vaulted floor where Campbell waited.

Campbell, dressed in a crisp gray suit with a vivid peacock tie, was at their window table, her nicotine-stained fingers drumming on the white linen cloth, blond hair slicked to one side. Three cigarettes had perished in a crystal ashtray. The restaurant was illuminated by futurist sconces like glowing fins on their dark granite columns. The walls and ceiling imitated the sky in airy artistic panels, with a vast painting of a jagged city breaking from a cloud bank occupying one wall, almost Biblical in its aspect. As he approached the table, Varnas gestured an ironic apology for being late. Sunlight flared against the silverware. Campbell was pulling another Lucky Strike from a silver cigarette holder when Varnas reached his seat, pushing his typewriter case beneath it.

Campbell took the water carafe in a pale, elegant hand and began pouring. "Here, Charles, have one of these."

Varnas spoke quietly, unfolding a napkin, noting a distilled faint of juniper from the glass, the atmosphere of alcohol burning at the rim like the corona of a transparent eclipse. "Gin? Oh, thank God." Silver embers scattered through him, bright as phosphor on a pin. The ice in his glass splintered pleasantly. There was a soft, expectant tremor in his fingers. "If I'd known you had gin, I might not have been late."

"But, if I'd told you, I couldn't have known if it was me or the booze that brought you."

Varnas imitated shock. "Darling…" The truth was that his ache for alcohol was ancient, archetypal. Something of his soul fluttered after it with a desire he found hard to articulate.

"Still, neither the police nor Ethyl Chaste—that's what I've decided to call the temperance ladies—will ever come up here."

Varnas drank again, a scintillating heat in his gums. "Poor bastards can't afford it," he said haughtily, bitterly. "Then again, neither can I."

"Do you like my hair?" Campbell said.

"Did you do something to it?"

"Swine." The aristocratic green of her eyes seemed to pulse once like a star glimpsed through stained glass.

"Yeah, I like it well enough," Varnas said. "It's short."

"Don't give me away."

"Of course not. I feel queer, though, Campbell."

"You bet you do." She made an obscene gesture with her cigarette and searched in her pocket for her lighter.

Varnas leaned across the table, his elbow settling into an empty bread plate. He glanced at the scene behind Campbell's padded angular shoulders, wreaths of smoke coiling about the noisy, suited tables, the men weaving like cobras in their seats, the waiters' jackets stiff as ancient ebony. Returning his gaze to hers, even in this androgynous disguise, she possessed the spectral radiance of a silent film. "It's really me who's in danger here," he said. "I'd like to bend you over."

"All in good time, Charles." Campbell lit her cigarette, snapping the lighter shut, and exhaling into Varnas' eyes, their English Channel blue enraptured under her shadowed breath. "All in good time."

Varnas coughed, lightly. "I don't see what's so good about time." He rested his temple against the cool pane of the window, unable to hear anything their waiter said when he arrived, merely gesturing his agreement with whatever Campbell ordered in that mannish voice she had cultivated to sustain her father's influence in forbidden places like this.

Manhattan spread out below them like an explosion, a metallic labyrinth of shrapnel and steam, fringed with piers that suggested the teeth of a warped cog. How long had Charles Varnas really been alive? He could not say. He did not believe in reincarnation, only that certain things, like the newspaper column coming to him on the street, suggested that he had more time than others. Somehow, he thought, he had not been born to die. He studied the thousands of men and women far below in the streets, submerged, bent, worn down by the malaise of falling money, walking under discolored Panama hats and sullen fedoras, women in cloche hats or headscarves, flecks of black faces down from Harlem in slouch caps. They seemed to walk on quicksand, suspicious of the ground beneath them, the dark drag, and coils of panic beneath the straight sidewalk.

A year ago, the Crash had come almost on the solstice, chewing at the heels of Hallowe'en when the dead come in like animals from the fields to hunger at stiff doors and gray frosted windows. Now, it was conceivable that the city was the place of permanent phantoms under the advent of a plague. The bone men picked at the air and chattered over somber collars, cupping their cigarettes out of the cold waves of the season. He imagined lines of emaciated women leaning into the breeze, trailing shrouds of rotten silk and nooses of matted fox fur, gangs of diseased children vanishing into the sewers to form a vengeful militia. Campbell refilled his glass, and he drank with the pleasant desperation that the first glass always set in him. The waiter returned to their table. Christ, he thought, I feel alive.

"Well, it seems that they still have some caviar left in Heaven," Campbell said, dropping the menu and appraising her new haircut in the back of a spoon. Pomade left a thumb-print.

Varnas stared at her, possessed by her radiance.

She spoke to him in her natural voice. "An aphrodisiac, no less. Come on, Charles. Somewhere in the Caspian, some poor sturgeon has injured feelings. Eat up." The last time she had dressed this way, she had worn a short-clipped wig, but now it was real. Then, her longer blonde hair had been damp with perspiration when he removed it in the descending elevator. She had put a 37 mm shell casing in her underwear to petrify him when he unzipped her trousers. Campbell was unaware of her place above the world, and he almost despised her for that carelessness. Her father's sequestered money seemed to have gone almost untouched by the disaster, but they were working their way through it without caution. If Campbell had ever possessed an image of her luck, only the faintest ghost of that knowledge haunted her now. A glamor of arrogance or defiance hung on her. Her smile was firm with ancestral confidence. Sometimes, Varnas wondered if she really believed in herself as fervently as she appeared to. He pricked himself for being so charmed by it, for all that.

Campbell spoke absently, "Hmm, I should have kept some clippings to make a mustache." Then, in seriousness, "Say, have you seen the herons down in Battery Park? They're quite disgusting! I don't know where they came from—" Observing his reverie, she struck Varnas on the knuckles with her spoon.

"Christ! Lay off."

"I can't tell if you're bored, or tipsy, with your head lolling on your neck like that. Like a handsome corpse in a stream." Campbell smiled, lost in some sudden premonition into which the city collapsed. She offered him a cigarette and he took it, resisting the instinct to reach into his pocket for his lighter to assist her. She was one of the gentlemen. If he wanted to enjoy this afternoon, he would have to sustain the illusion.

The pain in Varnas' hand was sharp.

"I'm sorry," she said. "Really, I am."

Varnas finished his gin and poured another. The rapped hand was unsteady in the echo of pain, so that he spilled a few drops. "Okay. Sure, conversation: You've been to a seance, right?"

"I never miss one," she said. She made a show of passing Varnas a napkin so that she could caress the bones her silverware had injured beneath it. "Are you looking for any particular ghost?" The more direct she was, the better her chance of diverting him.

Varnas shook his head. "No, I believe rather that one is trying to find me." Yet, the place he sought for that confrontation was blank. He looked from the window again, feeling the familiar vertigo of dreaming, and falling. Once more, the desert forced itself upon him. He glimpsed two figures lying on a bloody dune. It was the view a hawk might have, an aerial view of the necropolis, the gloomy tide of Cairo against the emptiness, the tombs where Varnas stalked, candle-blind, the red sun hanging over a nightmare of sand. Disembodied, he saw himself.

Inside the elevator, unfastening the fly of her gray pants, Campbell said, "I remember making love between the paws of the Sphinx."

"You could help me remember, Campbell."

"My line is in helping you forget," she said, unironically. How long ago was it? She was not sure, even though it had only been five years. "No more talk of ghosts. We've only got sixty seconds before the lobby."

Varnas reached for her as the Chrysler rose around them. He pushed the button that halted the elevator, jealous of time.

On Lexington Avenue, they walked without touching. Campbell glanced back at the shining building and its ornaments. "Birds of prey, made of aluminum."

"Aren't we just?" Varnas said and hailed a Yellow Cab with his briefcase. The sky was dark. "Evening has come early," he said. "Get home, I don't want anything to rain on your pomade. I'll see you, Campbell." They made a play of shaking hands. Varnas laughed. "I'll take the next one, don't worry."

"It's sweet of you to carry the typewriter around. You really don't have to for my sake—only if it's useful to you. I just thought it might help—" Help us, Campbell had wanted to say. "I'm sorry that I hurt your hand."

"You're lucky it wasn't my typing hand."

Varnas did not immediately hail a cab for himself when Campbell had gone. Instead, he paced the crowded sidewalk aimlessly, glancing occasionally at the sky, troubled by his fractured memory and the surrounding obscurity. It reminded him of awakening confused from a night with too many drinks, when he could feel thousands of silvery molecules in his skull trying to boil the blindness away, when he was afraid of what he might have said or done. What, he wondered, must happen in that fissure between absence and remembrance, before what one dreads returns like the pop of a flashbulb in a darkened room? He felt as though he were rehearsing for a scene that would occur there, yet the circumstances he could not imagine. At last, he gave up.

The man who drove Varnas' cab wore a leather overcoat and a cap, a heavy oval medal with his license number. His driving gloves almost concealed his arthritis, but his fingers twisted around the wheel like briar. His face, reflected in the windshield, was that of a man trying not to scream, drowning beneath a silent sheet of ice.

Such were the times, Varnas thought, since the money drained out of the world. His own money would be gone in another month, or before if he was not more cautious. Campbell wouldn't let him starve, but that wasn't the point. The thought of living through Campbell, through her father, appalled him. He had seen the scars from cigarette burns on Campbell's feet. Her father had done it to her, she explained. It was her father who had punished her with his red fingers the first time she menstruated. It was her father who kept her isolated and afraid, only gradually forming his ideas about how me might salvage something of her, drawing his plans like an astrologer his charts across great interplanetary gulfs and between the haunted stars. But her father no longer had a say in anything.

When Varnas considered it in the right light, Campbell's wasting of her inheritance was its own form of revenge. By the time the cab returned him to his apartment on Park Avenue, the rain was torrential.

THE VACATION

by

GARTH MIRO

1.

I'd gone mute. We were in line. It was hot. Yellow-y. She was the one who wanted to be here. I would've rather been in my chair, drinking beer in the cool. So, talking? No. I'd eat raw tip before that.

"Why are you always like this?" CC asked. Almost spat it up. "Hmm." I looked into the relentless, perfect-blue sky, sinking, sinking, about to crush us all. CC's beautiful eyes licking my skin. Searching for a spot turned brittle from line-sun where an insult might punch through.

To my core.

But too bad. I was already hollow down there. Decided. Just mechanically-separated sandwich ham and low-rent apartments and pressed oxy crumbs and nothing, that was my soul. Time without heroin: thirteen days, six hours, ten minutes, and thirty-three, thirty- four, thirty-five seconds.

"You have a massive ego problem, Hugo. All you American men do. You're a race of. . . "

I stopped listening. We were on vacation. The cruise ship beyond us, a swollen shaved belly—a barely-leaking metalloleviathan. The people, subnormals. My people. Soft-heads cut in two by overpriced blue light and glare light and UV and remorse and all bad vibe blocking sunglasses. Flabby bodies cased in gas station sandals and parrot-colored Bermudas.

It was a mass of mouths and hair and sweat and varicose veins and paunches and gonorrhea. A centipede of fake polite complaining, equipment. For me it was perfect.

I'd finally gone ahead and planned this thrice-requested trip, because my wife was fucking my boss. A suicide mission. Because my wife was also pregnant. And for the past month, every night, I'd been plagued by the same terrible dream: my unborn child being crushed to pale human paste by a massive uncircumcised Protestant cock. My boss, Robert Hauser III, went to one of those megachurches where grown men with goatees and ponytails try to live out some fantasy by playing drums on a stage, if that helps.

Not an ideal scenario.

The best possibility was that the thing was actually his and I was merely being tricked into raising a bastard. So, I was here to get to the bottom of it. Blow the case wide open. Cruise ships, even the big ones, aren't all that big. This particular outfit? They focused on "close-quarters for 'transforming connections.'" Whatever that meant. CC was slippery, smart. But from those words in the brochure it sounded like there would be nowhere for her to run and hide from my final confrontation, my avalanche of collected evidence, yes, for the next week plus two free days with the very limited-time package deal.

I noticed the guy ahead of us was really excited. Bouncing around like a toddler who needed to piss.

"Do you think they'll have a slide?" he whispered to his wife, unamused like most the others.

I pictured the two of them at the top of this imaginary waterslide, about to go down, his wife finally smiling and kicking him through the hole. Screams and blood spraying back out on her face. Like it was actually a woodchipper. Like she'd set it all up.

The sun continued dripping its pretty pink pulp

down our necks. My sweat had gone thick and beige and hateful. All parts under my clothes were quickly fusing into one pulsing organthing, which I dare not detail further. But I'd take it. I'd tolerate these hicks. And eat the thawing swill stored somewhere in the guts of the ship and sweat and do the goddamn limbo and much, much more. Important work was ahead.

And really, I didn't care about the cheating. I was doing the same. It was just that with CC, marriage was forever, she was still traditional about some things, the outward facing things, so I needed this evidence and plan to get myself out of the eternal contract. For a nice brisk marriage to a perky young woman-cheater, fine. But a whole eternity? Years and years and us both decomposing like these ones around us, with their constipation prescriptions and catheters, both only cheating worse and having to pile on more elaborate and ridiculous fictions just to cover our tracks?

Sounded like a lot of work. An entire stretch like that? And then after that? Hell, too?

Exhausting. No. We had to go our separate ways. She was much smarter than me, so I only had this window. Tap, tap, tap. (One of those sticks maestros used.) Paranoid trumpets, spill out your foam of music! Announce joyous doom!

"Welcome aboard!" a man—really more a boy-man with hyperwhite teeth and bleached hairwisps atop his balding dome—said.

We'd got to the line's front. Hmm. Don't think I'd ever seen someone so happy to be alive and working. Although it could have been plain old extreme fear; the two always looked indistinguishable to me. There above, hundreds of blank eyes stared down. One of them a window belonging to our future room on the ship. I stared back. You had to have confidence. This was it. My rancid princess of the seas. A trough for dregs. Here we go, I thought, sweating.

"And that's why you're never going to get a raise," CC continued. She'd been nagging the whole time. "To keep your ego all nice and shiny you've given up taking any real responsibility. Because then when it all goes to shit you can just shrug and blame the guy in the big chair. Rob isn't all that bad. He'll give you a raise if you just show him you're trying. But, no. Americans like you want to sit back with your cheap food, and TV, and wine—Californian 'wine', ha!—as someone else drives your life for you."

"I'm actually really glad we're doing this," I said. "You were right."

2.

Something had gone terribly wrong. This was nothing like the brochure. This room! Certainly not the, "Ritz of the Caribbean." Seeing the tacky little dump for the first time, fear started boiling up from CC's depths. I closed and locked the door behind us. A horrible wincing pain came from the unknown viscera to her cheeks. I put the bags on the bag thing. And she winced. Like she'd bit into a hotdog that'd grown a tumor. Hello there! She stepped back, slowly realizing our situation. Same. I did the same.

I stomped around like this, portraying these types of outrages were howling through my husbandhead. Tried my best to look confused. Holy—! The puke-obscuring burgundy carpet. The chair that faced nowhere. Nowhere! Table and lamp and TV remote all bolted down for maximum safety and insinuation.

At least we didn't have the cruise version of a bellboy pointing it out. Highlighting. That interchange always confused me. Never knew what to say. Here, sir, a closet. OK, clo-set, good. Here is the bed. Bed, ah, yes, I've seen one of those. Here is the toilet. For poop? Yes? Yes, sir. Poop and pee? Yes, all that, sir. Our econ-class hovel had only one small porthole window. It was only just above the sloshing sickly waterline, creating the lovely effect we were forever right at the beginning of drowning.

Inwardly, I smiled. I knew such "mistakes" induced

crushing identity crises in women like CC. Because to her, there were no mistakes. And maybe those-type people in line from before weren't just the maintenance people all showing up late, all at once, at the very same time. They were—were they—the other guests? Was this not one of those exclusive new cruises, with the clinking and cold apathy, the re-branded better ones her rich European friends bragged about, like she wanted? Like I promised!

No. She could smell it was something different. Lysol. Normal. In my mind, I donned a little bellboy hat and stuck out my arm. Here are people who rent furniture. Here is genuine enthusiasm.

Over buffets. Over de-shitted prawns. On ice. On credit. People who buy timeshares and physical copy porno. The sub-suburban. Wichita. Omaha. All of New Jersey. Like I said, my festering people! My repressed optimistic petty idiots! Now where's my tip bitch!

It all hit her. No, no. Since there were no mistakes and blood landed where it was supposed to, maybe this meant she was actually not one of the glittering seraphim. Face, reddening. Cruel au pairs and Klonopin lunches and Hermès riding saddles/dildos were perhaps not the accouterments of her paradise. Face, purpling. Because people got what they deserved. Now my eyes were licking her skin, which was much nicer. It was great! Although the chair that faced nowhere? A little strange, I'll admit.

"Did you really get the cheapest room?" she said, after recovering her classe superiore breath from the shock. Back to cool annoyance. Face, whitening.

"So this isn't like the rooms on the cruises out of Monaco?" I asked as stupidly as I could.

"Ha!" Was the final thought she had on the subject.

After that we had intercourse. This was the only way to describe the brisk obligatory deed it had become. For CC, merely something she performed to keep up the appearance she was still a part of the marriage. For me, another action to further usher my body towards death. A hammer being triggered on a million-chamber roulette revolver. One day the bullet would be there. If I fucked enough. If I kept going. It's the function of most marriages to lull us into letting go. Much easier to die with someone beside you, licking your balls.

We sat in silence, which I'm sure CC simultaneously loved and hated (she had the capacity), while I found the only TV channel that didn't cost twenty dollars an hour. A loop of the Cruise Director going over the daily schedule. His delivery was calm, almost serene. He was strangely saint-like. Maybe one of the lesser ones, though. Saint of Payday Loans or something. He had the same ultra white teeth as the boy-man employee from before. Very nice. A very intimate quality . . . how he looked straight into your eyes as he went down the list. Teeth shining. Never looking away. Looping. Or even blinking. Looping. Those lazy, gracious, aspic-blue eyes. I started getting drowsy. Couples workshop on Deck 5 . . . IND Spa session . . . bonding brunch . . . limbo . . . limbo . . . limb. . .

I shook my head and decided to go get drunk. CC followed out of spite. After four or five watery tequilas from the indoor piano lounge bar, she got fed up. "Jesus, Hugo," she said, and left to go find a massage.

It had been her recent submission—there was always some gob of pseudoscience she'd read in a magazine and was shoving in my face, always as if it were her own discovery—that I had become a raging alcoholic. And that such a constitution was bad. Really? In this economy? Well, I found it to be just the opposite.

I ordered another.

What CC truly hated was that American people thought it was some grave sin to have a glass of wine or two while pregnant. I actually agreed with her on this, let the little fucker have some fun, certainly that black amniotic Jacuzzi got boring. For her, the crowd decided everything in life. Society was the ultimate judge, and they were never wrong. Her trip would be agonizingly dry. And I knew this.

Naturally, my plan was to up my drinking considerably. Rub it in her face. I knew that if you got a pregnant woman mad enough, she'd say just about anything to hurt you. Pregnant women are the most honest creatures alive. You made me suffer, turned me into this, now it's your turn! I'd get her to confess everything, go into all the gory details just so she could smirk while she destroyed me. My evidence would be handed over willingly. CC was right. I had a massive drinking problem.

I suddenly felt something, which I did not yet understand. This helpful sinewy tension. Because ours was the cruise on the brink, that preceded the virus. The precipice of great change in the world that came to dock all leisurely ships. It caused a strange sort of electricity to swim through the air. Purplish, I thought then, as I emerged from the bar onto the main deck. I saw it in the sky. Like an anxious horny demon. Our metalloleviathan groaned in the dark water, under this electric-purple sky, because it knew what such a sky signaled. Death!

I looked out and saw we had already moved quite far from land. It was only a slit of glowing chaos. If you squinted, it actually looked kind of pretty.

THE WILDS

by

SARA DOTY

Prologue

The belly of Florida is a swamp, and I was born there, in the Wilds.

My birth season runs through the warm sconce of August, when the bougainvillea blooms and orange tree branches bow, weighed down with fruit; it's when you can hear cicada song rising up like steam from a swamp, rising to a harvest blue heaven, and magnolias fall to the earth like summer snow. Melony was born then, too. We shared a womb, fruit on vines braided together like wet hair, a ripe placenta pulsing between us like a collapsing star.

It's family folklore that I died for one minute when I was three years old, sixty seconds of oblivion. I was saved by my brother, revived by the Florida air. I don't know if it's accurate to say I was dead for a minute, that seems dramatic. After that my mother was suspicious, as if the absence of fear in my tiny body made me a liar, a snake in the grass.

"How are you so in love with swimming when you nearly died from drowning," she would snap. What my mother did not understand was that I was afraid, I am still, just not of water. Sometimes I imagine it. I'll see my three-year-old self tottering beside the swamp behind my childhood home, my hair still blonde, my face bright, touched. I would have leaned over the slope to the water's edge, unsteady on my pink, bare feet. Or maybe I had dived in, unabashed and brave. It must have been hot that day in August. Sometimes, too, I imagine that my mother pushed me.

The water would have been the murky dark of aventurine, foggy and strung with weedy veins. I must have struggled while slumbering gators and docile snakes remained stationary—that is because the Wilds would never let me die. It's likely my brother pulled me out amidst muck and lily pads, my mother watching as I vomited gray water onto my father's chest, my sister, Melony, crouching by his side. They thought I died, even my mother at first. That, at least, seems true. The Wilds swallowed me that day, embraced me like a parent, a protector. The Wilds would never harm me. It knows my name, it has known me before I was born. Yes, I am afraid, just not of water.

CHAPTER ONE:
THE CERULEAN MOUTH

I pull mulberries from low hanging branches in my father's backyard, a place that bleeds into swampland. I hand clusters of the black fruits to Marvel, my sister's daughter, who takes each offering by repeating a soft thank you, her head slightly bowed at my hip. Wind curls through the loblolly and sweet gum trees, whispering through the cabbage palms. The bald cypress trees look like kneeling druids in the shaded distance. The wetland pressed into the earth behind my father's house is a terrestrial planet of jade and salt, a viridian moon, another world to peer into. My sister, Melony, sits in the mulberry tree, her mouth moving in a constant, silent phrase, a scowl sinking her brows together, her bare feet dangling. Today she is in a hospital gown and nothing else. She has been dead four years now.

Marvel stores the berries in her shirt by holding the front hem up, forming a pouch, her belly button exposed. We're a safe distance from the swamp's edge that shudders breeze, but close enough to count the lily pads. Melony's ghost freezes, her mouth still, like she is waiting for something, listening, her hands grip the mulberry branches. I look away from her. If I stare at her ghost for too long my head will ache, like I'm glaring into the sun. I breathe in the scent of the world around me. The Wilds' hot air is sweet as sunlit magnolias, soil, and orange tree leaves. Marvel and I squish over fallen berry clumps. Juice stains our bare feet in bruised silhouettes, like bleeding beneath a top layer of skin, all in different shapes, but the same. Of the three mulberry trees in my father's yard, only one has grown tall and supple enough to give fruit. Marvel wants to know how old I am. My sister's ghost turns away, tired of watching us. I can see her dangling feet, glad her torso and head are shadowed.

"Guess how old I am," I say.

"Fourteen?" she asks and I laugh. "Sixteen?"

I tell her close. I am twenty-seven. Marvel is four. A breeze weaves through the cattails and pampas grass, making the piece of pristine sky visible in the distance glisten, and the water lap. We sit down on the ground cross-legged and sort all the berries into an eat pile on my lap and a discarded pile in the dirt. There is a lone gator in the swamp, at night you can hear it bellowing beneath black silt and balmy starlight. It's May. Mating season, my father will shrug whenever bloated grunts curl inside the house from the humid air outside, but he's wrong. I can recognize what a lonely cry is, what it feels like in your breast, that sensation of reaching out a hand, even though you know, you know, nothing is coming. The gator hisses and roars from its throat, its heart a drum, a clock, a weight bearing down. It makes my chest want to open and sing. Marvel and I consume the blister-thin fruits together, juice runs down our chins. The trees shudder, the gator slumbers, and the Wilds sings around me. I lick the juice off my fingers and Marvel copies me. I tell her I could eat that shit all day and she gasps, then laughs. My father steps off his back porch. He thumps over to us, blocking out the sunlit green, that sky of trees. The left side of his mouth droops. He looms there, like a wraith, hovering above the ground.

"Swamp's dryin' up." My father juts out his chin. My sister's ghost leaps off the tree and fades from view before she can hit the ground. She would never miss a chance for a dramatic exit, even if I am her only audience.

"So am I." I let the words hide under me as I stand, I let them stay in the dirt. Marvel gets up too, her face and fingers glisten with sticky mulberry, her yellow shirt ruined. He says something about getting Marvel cleaned up for dinner. There is a pause, even Marvel stays still. He wants me to do it, give her a bath, put her in pajamas, brush her hair. I ignore him and look out at the swamp, feeling the sleeping gator. Marvel walks to the porch. Father and I follow. I'll be back, I whisper to the Wilds.

Inside the chill from the air conditioner is jarring, like stepping in snow, it sucks the Wilds right out of my skin. My father has a spacious and overpriced terracotta house in a manicured suburb. The smell of coffee grounds and mildew on paper overwhelms my senses, everything chemically cool and electric blue. Stacks of old books line the far-left wall, they were not here the last time I was here.

"Where did the books come from?" I ask the back of my father as he heads down the hallway, holding Marvel's hand. She's whining about taking a bath. He does not hear me. I make myself a tequila with ice from the bar cart positioned between the kitchen and the living room. There are no dirty dishes lingering around the sink, but there are canned goods stacked on the counters, piles of mail unopened, two dozen empty mason jars. The house is slowly slipping into disrepair.

The old books stacked like towers are thick with yellowed pages, I pick one up, interested until I read the cover, *Whose Who in the Bible*. I set it down, and pick up the next, *The Rapture, the Reaping, and the End of Times*, and another *Understanding Evangelicalism, a Divine Document*. There must be a hundred crumbling texts with the same theme. I wonder if my father is holding these books for his church.

Wholly uncurious now, I sit on the couch and sip my drink. Being in this house makes me think of my mother, Madalin. Tequila gnaws at the crawling feeling under my skin, my teeth throb from the ice. I think of the mother wound, about the pain my grandma Lilith passed down to my mother, and then the pain Madalin passed to me, my inheritance I carry around like a tumor in my breast. I hear Marvel scream at my father, all I can make out is Mama. Melony appears on the couch beside me, her eyes bore into mine, beseeching me. A familiar sensation of self-loathing seeps into my first layer of skin, sinking past it into my subcutaneous layer, and then, to my muscles before it reaches down deep to the glittering, umber marrow.

My therapist Jane claims I need to use the tactics she teaches me to end the negative self-talk that replays in my head in a loop. She works under the cognitive-behavioral model of therapy and likes to wear matte lipstick in nude shades while she quotes Aaron Beck at me. She likes to mention anecdotes about her diets while wearing nylon, a therapist who, it seems, has never suffered anything worse than a cheating lover, a grumpy divorce, and who wants me to just love myself, already. She meets all the conventional beauty standards for women, skinny, slight curves, blonde, tiny bird knees, a young, almost childlike face, prominent breasts. She uses phrases like positive self-affirmation, maladaptive thought patterns, cognitive restructuring, inner child work, and emotion mapping, all while glancing at her reflection in the dark wall clock over her couch.

Currently Jane wants me to participate in inner child work, she was delighted when I explained my mother wound. A vulnerable moment for me, and therefore, a breakthrough. She believes that working with my inner child will solve everything. Everything. I want to abandon Jane, but when I imagine life without therapy, I see grandma Lilith falling from a window. Her body will change to Madalin's, and finally, it's me plummeting to the ground, all in spaces of blinks, between breaths, a rapid succession, Lilith, Madalin, then me— Lilith, Madalin, me. My skull cracks on the sidewalk, what's inside of me pops out of all my facial orifices, my tangled spine protrudes from my shoulder. I stay with Jane.

Jane wants me to hang a baby picture of myself next to a mirror and talk to it like it is a child that I love. She wants me to walk around with dozens of my baby pictures stuffed in my pockets, fistfuls of them, like a little boy with baseball trading cards packed for use at a moment's notice. Every time I feel self-hatred, I am to whip out these pictures and speak kindly about/to myself. It is relentless. Mapping is an even more bizarre technique that Jane is excited about, and, like inner child work, it aims to make me feel like a child in my body.

Emotion mapping is all about discovering why a stimulus provokes an out of place arousal. In Jane's words, if you feel a loud emotion that does not fit the situation, then it's because you did not process something in your childhood, and now it's wreaking havoc in your life. Inside my dad's house I feel six years old. I feel self-hatred everywhere. Was six the first time I ever felt this? Mapping is a foggy experience of following thoughts backward, like I am a cartographer drawing the connecting roads and mountain ranges, until I can step back and see an origin, the first time I ever felt shame or rage or envy.

I drain my glass as Marvel's muffled voice trips up into a song. The shower turns on. Singing pushes out into the hallway and the electric whir of the water heater turns on.

I make another drink. My father has a framed picture on

his mantle. I crunch on an ice cube, studying the old family photo. It's the five of us on Easter morning, Mel and me in frilly, mint dresses, flanking our older brother, Haimish, his body already too tall for his dress pants and jacket. We're in front of our parents, my father, pre-stroke, fat then, and happy, and my mother, shriveled and skinny, beaming in a pink suit. She looks like she just finished a fit of laughter, the mirth bit down in her cheek. I remember that Easter, it was the year before my mother had her DUI charge, two years before she left. It's creepy my dad has this out, it wasn't up last time I was here. The tequila gives me the confidence to turn the picture around so I don't have to look at it.

My mother moved out when I was eleven. It was like she died. She never called. Haimish always doubles down on this—she never called. Now she lives at Core Pines Assisted Living Facility in Jacksonville. She leapt from a window to kill herself the year I started college, I heard about it from my dad who kept these weird tabs on her, they never formally divorced. Madalin's jump only succeeded in oversaturating her brain with blood. She no longer speaks or eats, and lives like a vegetated baby. Haimish calls this poetic justice. Pansy, my mother's sister, and who Haimish calls the Madalin Apologist, calls this a deep tragedy. I don't call it anything. My grandmother died by jumping out a window. She was successful in her attempt whereas Madalin is now drooling in her lap for the unforeseeable future, perhaps thirty more years. After the bizarre novelty of it wears off, it is almost comical that Madalin wanted to die in the same way her mother died, like a family tradition (we all try and kill ourselves by falling from windows, no exception, no pistols in mouths, or swallowing 150 milligrams of trazodone, only swan dives from high rise breakfast nooks). It makes me wonder if I will eventually do the same.

My best friend in college, Venn, who majored in mortuary science and funeral services, once told me that human beings are like books, their lives are stories, hundreds of narratives collected in skin. I agree with him, humans are like stories, but I don't think they are like books; they're maps. Venn lives two hours north of Jacksonville, in Found Creation, Georgia, still in our college town, like he's a fixed origin point.

My father walks into the living room, a glass of bourbon already in his hand, Marvel peers out from the hallway in her pajamas, her face scrubbed pink. I glance down at my tequila, annoyed my father has a glass of alcohol too. Marvel comes over and crouches at my feet. She puts her wet head in my lap. Melony's ghost is gone again. My father flips the framed picture on the mantle around and says nothing. In my mind's eye, my mother takes on the form of Lot's wife, the woman who was turned to a pillar of salt for looking back at a crumbling Sodom. Depending on the version of the Old Testament you read, the city was on fire. Except this Madalin version of Lot's wife in my head does not look back. She goes free and I am the one turned into salt, left to burn beside a destroyed city. I stay up with Marvel in the living room until it's time for my father and her to do their nighttime prayer routine. I step outside, the gator's song sobbing in the muggy air. I stay out there, cloistered by the Wilds until I am heavy, and my head falls back against the mulberry, and I can't keep my eyes open. I sleep in the guest room at the back of the house with the window open. Frogs and crickets and the steaming Wilds all lulling me into sleep, the lone gator purrs. The moon looks like a sliver of an opalite fingernail.

The next morning I leave my father's house, southbound, the world still purple dark and street lamped. Melony's ghost sits in the passenger seat, gazing fitfully out the window, her mouth motionless. I drive until the highway smooths into a treeless horizon of blue, the sun slowly blooming.

The beach is full of young families, twenty-some-thing moms and dads hovering around flashy toddlers. I only brought my car keys and the musty quilt I keep in my trunk for this exact purpose. I feel seventeen. I spread out the blanket so I can lay back and doze under a brilliant sky.

Mapping backward in a dazed dream I remember when Melony and I got baptized. It was on my father's birthday, I was five years old. My father wore his maroon suit and matching tie, my mother wore a maroon cat dress with shoulder pads. I remember stepping onto our back porch with Mel to show my father the white, shapeless gowns we were to be baptized in, his birthday present. That afternoon was balmy from the heat mingling with jasmine and hanging wisteria. My father's eyes shimmered like silver clouds, he rested his Cuban cigar on the patio table. He said we looked like little angels.

At the church our pastor held me like a baby in the clear tank elevated behind the stage he preached on every Sunday, while Mel waited for her turn in a tiny changing room behind the chapel. He asked me three questions, the way a troll might before he lets you pass a bridge in a fairy tale. He dunked me backward, and I did not cough or splutter when I rose. I stood up in the tank and raised both my arms, the pastor's huge hand rested on the crown of my skull. The congregation erupted in applause, their faces contorting in roars of joy, their claps and cheers undulating in the sanctuary, their mouths frothing, until they no longer were a sea of human faces. They were animals, stomping, snorting, and rearing. I could see my father in the front row, he was laughing and crying at the same time, jumping up and down. My mother looked like she was dancing, digging into the ground.

Under the heat of the washed-out violet sky, my skin has tinged pink. The ocean speaks to me, it's all I can hear, the great inhalation and exhalation of the sea. I walk through the waves into the salty billows that look crested in starlight under the sun, swaths of clear, iridescent silk. I pause when the slapping waves are above my belly button and below my breasts, rocking me back and forth like a tree in the wind. I glance back at the shore. Melony is standing on the beach, watching me. I lay back and float for a space of time.

I emerge from the shore, glistening, my eyes stinging and my head clear. I collapse on my musty quilt, exhausted and baptized. I lay back, a roaring in my ears, I am clean. The Wilds is the only thing that can absolve me.

Later that afternoon, I return to my father's house and I sit on the porch swing on the front veranda, listening. Marvel is still at preschool. I want to see her before I leave. The alligator bellows in the distance, mournful and heavy, the leaves in the dwarf maples and live oaks shiver. My father stomps out to the porch and spits into the wilting beds. Some stray wisteria grows from a maple branch onto the porch's ceiling. His gutters are filled with Spanish moss.

"Waiting for Marvel?" he asks.

"Yeah."

"She loves you," he says.

"I know that."

"I know you know that." He coughs. "I know you know a lot of things..." He clears his throat. "I think you know what you need to do, Sam." I don't say anything for a long time, years in three minutes. The silence feels like pricks of needles on my vertebra. Steam collects in the air, heat rises off my shoulders in waves that bend light around me. I know what he is going to ask, and I hate him in a place that seers my insides, my chest and stomach, where I hold back a boiling ocean all the time. My dead sister appears in the grass, her mouth moving rhythmically, constantly, reciting her mantra. She walks up the sun-bleached steps, the veranda's blue paint is peeling. My father's eyes shimmer.

"I know that you need to paint this porch," I say. "I could help you paint it."

"Melony—I mean, Sam." My dad sighs. "Sorry, I am getting old." My sister's ghost sits on the railing, her back to both of us. Sometimes it's not an accident. He wants me to be her, wants me to wear her skin. If he could he'd flay Melony's corpse and have me wear it, a skin coat for me to don so I can pretend to be Marvel's mother and his favorite daughter. My anger breaks into something livid and alive. The ghost of Melony flickers, like a light bulb going in and out, the sounds of the Wilds around me dims. I feel like I am ascending, my stomach floating to my lungs. My dad says something, but it's like a voice in another room.

In the distance the sky is melding to a deep iron. Marvel's pre-k school bus parks at the end of the driveway, we all watch her small form emerge from the steps. My dad raises one hand in the air until the doors shut. Marvel runs to the porch, her cheeks flushed and her ponytail loose. Thunder muffles in the distance, the sky between the thunderheads and above me is deepening to a satin, steel-eye blue. I stand to greet her and she runs into my arms.

"Can you stay one more night?" Marvel asks. I see my dad's face over her warm head that smells of playground sweat and artificial strawberry from her shampoo.

"No, I can't, turtle dove," I tell her. She makes a huff

sound. My dad is shrunken, helpless, the husk of a roach. I am the daughter of insects, of mentally ill pigs, a shattered vase that can't hold its waters. What everyone says about Madalin, that she is victim to her own mind, a prisoner in her body now, I don't buy it, I don't. Mothers who abandon their daughters don't get sympathy from me.

"I want to come with you," she howls, and then she begs. I leave her to suffer her big emotions all alone on the porch. My dad slouches next to my car, his arms crossed over his chest.

"Maybe consider staying one more night," he mumbles. I almost laugh.

"Can't," I say, and he visibly sags with desperation. He stands close to me, like he wants to embrace me but can't.

"I think it would do you good to see Madalin, I really do, it might help with closure, might help you, you know." He trails off.

"You're crazy if you think that, Dad."

"Mel—I mean Sam, I don't understand none of this, just none of it." He turns away and squints in the light. I tense my shoulders. He did it again.

"Let's not do this," I say in a forced calm. Melony's ghost materializes beside me.

"Sam. You cannot continue living this way."

"I said I do not want to hear this, Dad."

"I want to talk about this, Melony. Ah, sorry. Sam. I meant to say Sam."

My anger rises again, only this time I let it free. My body levitates, my limbs contort, my face peels back to expose what waits beneath, my mask slipping. I scream in a joyful, bright rage, it bursts from my chest, exploding out between my twin lungs, expelling everything onto the driveway, out in the open air. I pull my hair, I smack the side of my head, my cheeks, but it's not enough. I dig my fingernails into my cheeks and drag them down, clawing. I do the same to my arms. I scream over and over not to *fucking* call me that. Don't ever fucking call me Mel again. The Wilds press around me, I inhale it like smoke, like a drug, a scent I need to survive. Marvel runs off the porch, her tiny legs quick and small like a spider's. Her hair is free from the ponytail, it whips behind her like a banner. My father does not let her get to me. He picks her up and she struggles, her arms outstretched. It's not the water I'm afraid of.

"I want to go with you!" Marvel bleats like a lamb, broken. My father places her down and she buries her face behind his knees.

"I know Madalin leaving messed you up," my father says, real tears in his eyes. The sight of him crying makes me nauseous, both from my disgust of him, and of myself. "It messed all of us up, Haimish even..." Thunder rattles the Wilds' spine. "But you can't let that keep you from her, you're—"

I rear back and slam my head against the car door to make it stop. The Wilds curls around me, its warmth pressing against my skull, my chest is an inflating balloon. *Flee*, the Wilds whisper like the wind braiding through leaves and grass and cloud, *Go now, come back later. Later,* voice like god in the trees.

My head spins and my thoughts are slow, sluggish. Wind blows my hair around my head. I feel seventeen, about to escape.

"Melony is dead." I hiss, like a hawk pinning its wings together and diving down for the kill. I open the car door and get in, my head still spinning. I plug the key into the ignition. My cheeks and arms burn where I raked my nails in, my forehead pulses. He pushes Marvel away from his legs, off the driveway to give me room, and she soothes herself by sniffling and chewing her hair, crouching like a wounded animal, her cries quiet and contained. I put the car in reverse and pull out of his driveway so fast my bumper scrapes the asphalt from the curb. Melony's ghost appears in my rear-view mirror. At a stop light I glance back, her mouth moves in her silent mantra, it's the only thing she ever tries to tell me.

I am like Lot's wife, too, leaving a crumbling city on fire behind me. And I do not look back, just like her. I can't. Melony continues her silent chant. We are twins, a broken branch of the same tree, only, one is without her skin, and the other is without her name. It's not the water I'm afraid of.

They're going to find out. She mouths, rocking gently, *they're going to find out.*

CROCODILE MAN

by

DAVID LUNTZ

CHAPTER 1

The moment Jimmy sent the bank teller into the afterlife, he was thinking about Thomas Hobbes' political advice to future rulers: "The passion to be reckoned upon is fear." But now Jimmy's wondering whether Hobbes got it wrong, because the crazy bitch bleeding out against the wall sure wasn't afraid of having a .357 shoved in her face.

Jimmy ambles out the bank, throws the bag of cash onto the front passenger seat, and drives off. He turns on the radio, flipping through the talk stations. There's the usual crap about troll farms, cellphone radiation, microchips in vaccines, and alien colonization. Some guy's bragging about burning books. Then he's saying, "Death kills so much 'cause death's just upping his game so he can take out time. And time's a fish that won't stop drinking until the ocean's dry." It sounds oxymoronic to Jimmy but also makes a weird kind of sense.

Jimmy figures he'll think about it more later. He heads to his favorite diner right off the 405 on Venice Boulevard. After a bank job he likes to treat himself to a big stack. He likes the waitress there, too. She's heavyset. Jimmy likes big women. Her eyes exude a tide of sadness that Jimmy could wade into and float out on forever. She reminds him of the sixteen-year-old girl he had an insane crush on as a teenager who one day vanished when her dad got transferred to another job. Jimmy likes to think of the waitress as that same girl just grown up. She's making serious eye contact. Jimmy wishes he'd never taken a vow of chastity. Killing's aroused him. But if a man makes a vow and breaks it, then he can't look himself in the mirror. Such a man becomes invisible to himself.

He leaves a big tip and heads off to get some gas. The attendant is a young know-it-all jerkoff whining about forest fires in Malibu and climate change. Jimmy hates people like this and vaguely thinks of wasting him, though he does believe in climate change. He'd once read about how crocodiles swam off the coast of Alaska fifty million years ago, how it was all tropical and lush there. Then he read about how certain rats kill crocodiles by entering their mouths when the crocs are sleeping. How they eat their way right through them. That's when Jimmy knew how they could get him: water rats. It's the only thing that scares him. Because deep down Jimmy knows what he really is.

The gas guy's given Jimmy bad vibes. He doesn't like thinking about rats. Jimmy reckons taking the canyon route will suck up the negative energy. From the 405 he switches onto Mulholland. As he comes over the crest, the spring sky's deep blue clang breaks his heart. Out in the distance, the blinking ocean strikes some ancient chord that tells him to "come home." He turns the radio back on. Another asshole's talking about breeding red heifers for sacrifice on the Temple Mount because he's calculated the exact moment the Rapture will occur. All based on his close reading of the Book of Daniel. Jimmy thinks, *it's like being in some amnesiac stupor, hearing the same joke over and over, because humanity went brain dead after the eighteenth century and all we can do now is fuck dead metaphors.* But he's biased. Because when he's not pulling bank jobs or doing freelance wet work, he collects first editions of the works of Hobbes, Locke, Hume, and Descartes. He's got them displayed on handmade teak shelves above his drawers of Glocks, vintage Mausers, Berettas, Magnums, Uzis, grenades, and a large cache of ammo.

His burner phone buzzes on top of the blood-specked duffle bag in the passenger seat. He pulls over into the emergency lane. Wipes the phone on his jeans and takes the call.

"Yeah."

The voice is slurry like it's coming through water.

"Got a job for you. Special delivery. Needs careful handling."

It's Ricci. His 'booking agent.'

"Uh-huh," Jimmy says

"Twenty K for a trip across town. Near the port."

"What's the package?"

"Can't say. Just got an address."

Jimmy knows it smells. But there's a rare edition of Robert Hooke's *Micrographia* he's bidding on. Now, with Ricci's offer, he's sniffing the calfskin, musty pages, vinegary ink, and dry straw on the floor of its birthing press. Then, soaring off on an imaginary thermal, he sees below the glittering serpentine folds of the Thames, all the glory of Robert Hooke's, Samuel Pepys', and Christopher Wren's London before the Great Fire of 1666 crisped it.

"Fifty," Jimmy says.

"Done."

Jimmy pulls out his smartphone from the glove compartment and opens a mobile wallet app. Watches the crypto hit.

The burner phone pings.

An address and time sit in the text box.

Another ping.

"Text back when you got the package for forwarding info. Pickup code is: "So began outrage from lifeless things."

Jimmy deletes the message, takes out the SIM card, and tosses the burner phone out the window. Watches it bounce down a culvert on the side of the highway exploding in rainbow shards. He stares at the fading colors for a few moments figuring there's a metaphor somewhere in there.

*

Jimmy gets back on the 405 then switches to the 101 into North Hollywood where he lives on a top floor of a brick condo that used to be a bakery. He puts the cash in a safe and downs a few Buds while cleaning his gun. Then takes a nap.

Six hours later, he pulls up to the address in Ricci's text. It's a stucco house in Torrence, 1940s vintage, product of a boom time and bygone era of easy credit and optimism. Most of the other houses on the street are abandoned or boarded up. Terra cotta tiles, white paint, Moorish curves, Valencia orange trees. Supposed to evoke some kind of Iberian nostalgia. Stars smoke through evening sky in burnt sienna and magenta wisps. Air's laced with desert pine, creosote, and jacaranda.

Jimmy's gone very still. Hyper vigilant. His heart beats at the resting pace of a marathon runner's. It's how he gets before a job. Maybe it's a gift. Without seeing, he sees the cars there, their license plates, dents, and hubcaps, collates all the shadows moving in the dying light. Like his mind is some super-absorbent daguerreotype soaking up all movement. But not much is moving here. Which is bad. Bad like dogs not barking bad in more than one sense.

Jimmy figures the place is some kind of flophouse, whorehouse, or safe-house. Maybe a combo of all three. And whatever package they got inside is smoldering and in desperate need of cooling motion: maybe meth, fentanyl, high-end designer-synthetic shit… but most likely a fresh corpse. Some inconvenient witness due to testify and in need of disappearing. Figures this got to be it, given Ricci's desperation.

He checks his watch. Showtime. Scans the house once more. Blinds drawn. No shadows. Grips his .357 because everything about this job is wrong and everything in him screams, *Get. Out. Now.* But he took the money. It's the same thing as taking a vow.

*

The buzzer is an ivory circle in a black box. He presses it with his knuckle. Hears steps pounding inside. Wood floor. From the sound of the pounding, Jimmy reckons what's coming at him is just shy of three hundred pounds and six feet high. He pulls his Desert Eagle .357 out from behind his back. Tightens his jacket over his double-reinforced Kevlar vest.

"Yeah," a voice grunts behind the door.

"Here for the package."

"Got some ID?"

Jimmy says, "So began outrage from lifeless things."

Door opens.

An empty hallway gapes before Jimmy. He freezes. In the circular wall mirror at the end of the hallway, Jimmy catches the reflection of the guy moving out from behind the door and a sawn-off swinging his way. Jimmy jumps out to the side of the entranceway just as the scorch of the muzzle flash singes his hand. Most of the shot sprays wide. Jimmy hears the click of a reload, steps toward the door and fires three times. The guy grunts and falls face down in front of the doorway. Jimmy kicks him back into the hallway and slams the door shut. Most of the guy's chest is gone and half his head is hanging on his neck.

A plum juice puddle forms from under his shirt and spreads across the floor. Jimmy sticks his piece in the back of his jeans, picks up the shotgun and goes into a crouch. He knows there's someone else in the house.

The hallway is the leg of a T that leads to two other rooms. Cigarette smoke's coming from the left room, so at the end of the hallway, Jimmy extends the shotgun blindly into the space of the right room and fires. Hears a wheeze like a leaking tire and a thud like a wet cement bag falling onto the wood floor. *Gotcha.* Jimmy sets the gun down and pulls out his Desert Eagle. Steps into the other room. Big mistake. The fatal kind. On a table he sees an ashtray with three cigarettes. He leaps back into the cover of the hallway. Too late. Two bullets slam into his chest like a sledgehammer.

He's on his back, squirming. Light blazing in his eyes, like a star getting shredded in a black hole. He thinks the edge of the moon smells like lemon. His mouth tastes like it's stuffed with spiderweb balls. But through the sensory confusion, Jimmy's in a deep state of calm. A calm so deep he's surprised by it. Like he's been split in two and is watching himself in a movie. All while another part of himself is trying to work out what the fuck is going on. Because time isn't moving right and he's thinking that David Hume was spot on about the impossibility of finding true causes for effects. And John Locke got it massively wrong about people being born as 'blank slates' because he's located enough of an untaught knowledge to survive this ambush and blast four rounds into the guy standing above him.

Jimmy watches the man slump down against the wall in a kind of ecstasy, like he's having an opium dream.

*

The fireworks will get some 911 calls going. Jimmy reckons he's got about five minutes to sweep the place before the Five-O show. Puts on some latex gloves, goes into the kitchen, finds a plastic shopping bag and starts picking up his shells, the dead guys' cellphones and wallets. On the table with the cigarettes, there's a large manila envelope. Picks it up and pulls out two photos of himself. Throws it in the bag. Then he hears some sobbing coming from the first room he cleared. Jimmy steps into the room. Gun cocked. The sobbing's coming from a closet behind the dead guy. Jimmy yanks the door open. It's a boy. No more than six, large creamy-olive eyes. Probably Mex, hands flex-cuffed.

The boy whispers, *Ayúdame, Ayúdame, por favor.*

An alien sensation ripples through Jimmy. Like the kid were some time-warped mirror that's kept Jimmy's reflection for thirty years. A scared kid with nothing to protect him but his own grit. Now he's calculating all the variables the unexpected presence of this child has presented. The smart move would be to cap the kid because the kid can ID him. And Jimmy figures the kid is as good as dead, anyway. But Jimmy's never killed a child. And his soul's worn down enough from all the people he's killed, screwed over, and abandoned that if he kills this kid, he knows his soul will be shredded beyond repair.

He takes out his boxcutter, cuts the flex-cuffs, and says to the shaking boy, "*Ven conmigo.*"

*

The boy is in the front seat next to him.
They're back on the highway heading west.
The boy's sucking his thumb.
Jimmy says, "*¿Hablas íngles?*"

Kid shakes his head.

"*¿Dónde están tus padres?*"

The boy takes his thumb out and says, "*Muertos.*"

Jimmy nods and thinks, *Yeah, mine too.* The kid's an orphan now, bound to become part of the system. Jimmy thinks maybe he should have done him a favor and saved him from that horror with a merciful shot to the back of the head. Catching him in the mirror, Jimmy relives the terror and confusion of growing up in the foster system, which he'd managed to escape mainly by running away, skipping classes, and haunting the local community college library. By the time he was sixteen, he'd gone through ten families, all the Greek myths, and most of the required texts for a graduate degree in modern philosophy, English, and European history.

Yet his Harvard and Yale wasn't a rundown library, but a graffiti-covered Korean War-era school bus. On the other side of the window's grime-specked divide, he filled the broken streets with the worlds of Homer, Aeschylus, and Virgil. The hustlers playing Three-card Monte on orange crates turned into "long-haired Argives and Danaans." Pimps, dealers, and jivers sucking away on bullhorn-sized spliffs, were ringers for Achilles's swaggering Myrmidons. *Colombianas*, with their bow-shaped ship launching lips, strutting with confidence they'd never go hungry, were his Helen of Troy.

Until one day Jimmy got tired of those foolish replacements, got off the bus, and went up to a man playing Three-card Monte and said, "Show me how you do it. I want to know." The man told Jimmy to "fuck off," and then beat him into a pulp when Jimmy didn't. Jimmy kept coming back. He didn't know why. He just knew he had to understand this world. That a certain part of his schooling was over and this man was the next step in his education. And then one afternoon the man sighed, told Jimmy he was a "dumb fucking burro," and guided him through the full-hustle curriculum. The man's name was Hector and on the day when he had nothing more to teach Jimmy, said, "But my friends call me 'Ricci.'"

Jimmy left his foster home and started doing bigger jobs for Ricci and his associates. Heists, shakedowns, managing a stable of undocumented teen drug dealers, and occasional disposing of persons causing other people headaches. At twenty-five, his luck ran out. He got arrested for murder. But the body was never found. So, he copped to a ten-year plea for the lesser charges of unlawful possession and B&E.

In jail, a priest who'd gotten a doctorate on the seventeenth-century Cambridge Neo-Platonists before finding his calling as a "prison father," introduced Jimmy to that era and its works. When Jimmy got out (seven years for good behavior), he'd begged Jimmy to go to college and continue his studies. When Jimmy declined, the priest consoled himself that Jimmy's decision was just God working in His mysterious ways. But Jimmy's decision was not mysterious. He'd gone back to Ricci because Ricci was the closest thing to an older brother and father Jimmy ever had.

Now, he's trying to piece the puzzle together. He figures the kid was abducted because his mom or dad or both saw something they shouldn't have. Maybe the kid did, too. But something got fucked up, except Jimmy just doesn't know what. He just knows that Ricci set him up to take the fall. That's why Ricci was so quick to pay him. Fucking sold him out.

Jimmy laughs, screams, and sobs. Bangs the steering wheel. *So, it was just tit for tat for Ricci the whole time. Nothing more. Transactional. Like pilot fish who eat the parasites off sharks. Or plovers that fly into crocodiles' mouths and clean their teeth. Fuck you, Ricci. I never ratted on you. Gave you seven years.* Some riptide surges inside Jimmy, he guns the engine and heads back on the 405.

He sees her coming out the diner heading toward him in the parking lot. Her shift is done. Still wearing her uniform and name tag. Jimmy gets out with the kid. He's holding the boy's hand. Her eyes light up in surprise when she spots him. Good surprise, not just because he left a good tip.

"Hi," Jimmy says with a big smile.

"Hey there, nice to see ya again," she says.

"I need some help. Kid here needs some watching tonight. Maybe a nice meal. Found him in a bad situation. Don't speak much English."

He pulls out an envelope.

"Here's ten grand for your trouble. I'll swing by tomorrow, pick him up, just got to take care of something now."

Jimmy knows he's really asking her to commit herself to him in a way much deeper than babysitting a strange kid. That he's asking her to leap off some unknown cliff with him hoping there's a deep cool lake below to catch their fall. But maybe she understands way more than Jimmy gives her credit. She looks at him for a moment, takes the envelope of cash and nods.

Her eyes tell him a decision's been made.

They say: *Yes, I do.*

*

Jimmy reloads his Desert Eagle and gets back on the highway headed towards Ricci's home out near Anaheim. Passes by freight yards, eighteen wheelers, fast food joints, and gas stations. Energy going in a million different directions and destinations. Pulsing lights from planes circling over LAX weave themselves into a bracelet dangling from Orion's ankle; moonlight swimming in stagnant tar pools sublimate into the river Lethe; downtown city blocks fold into the Minotaur's labyrinth; barge drivers out on the dark bay, ferrymen... He's doing it again, the substitution game, because after prison he thought he could do both, lead a stickup life and one of learning, too.

He's terrified to let it go because it's all he knows and he's made it all his. But now he thinks about the kid, about her, and thinks maybe he'd got it all wrong. Like maybe he could learn how to live with others, even if he has to break his vows. Become something else. Create new vows.

THE BRIGHTEST FLAME

by

VALERIE PALMER

FORMER WEST BERLIN, 1992

The past few weeks, the days had blurred together. Aleksandr would wake at 7:30, leave the apartment in Charlottenberg at 8:35, work at Ivan's warehouse, return to the apartment at 7 or 8 at night, eat Chinese take-out, watch television, and then go to bed. The next day, Aleks would repeat this process. And the next day. Those early mornings in the backseat of Ivan's car, racing down Berlin's boulevards, gave Aleks a brief glimpse of freedom. Commuters buttoned up in thick wool coats and wrapped in scarves stood at bus stops, waiting. For a second, Aleks locked eyes with a striking brunette in a blue coat, standing at a corner, waiting to cross Danckelmannstrasse. Children struggled under the weight of enormous backpacks on their way to school. Adults walked briskly down sidewalks. "Time is money," Ivan would say as his foot pressed the gas, urging the car a single breath from the bumper in front of them.

Ivan had transferred Aleks to a new project in the warehouse, which meant he no longer sat in that windowless back room all day humming sonatas with his friend Dimitri, also a musician. Aleks now worked in a large open space, where men with ruddy complexions and calloused hands hunched over wide tables assembling devices that involved metal brackets and wires. He appreciated getting out of that stuffy back room and being in the middle of activity even if the other men resisted his attempts at conversation. Aleks wondered how they had made it from Russia to Berlin. He'd get a nod or a glance in response to a comment, but then a long silence would squelch the possibility of conversation.

Every morning, small cargo trucks from the East pulled up at the back door, their drivers glassy-eyed from days of traveling on cheap Communist concrete riddled with deep potholes and jagged cracks. Men with thick chests and muscled arms unloaded cardboard boxes from the truck's cargo, stacking the brown boxes on dollies and wheeling them down the hall and into a storage room. The drivers, exhausted, would sit down to a plate of potatoes and minced meat dumplings, devouring everything in an instant, and then disappear into a large utility closet to sleep. One of his first days working in the front of the warehouse, Aleks had opened the wrong door in his search for a bathroom. The slit of light from the hallway illuminated a row of cots, where men slept cocooned in blankets.

Aleks' new task involved placing a "Made in West Germany" label on the lower right-hand corner of a small plastic bag. He applied the gold sticker with its red border, the size of his tiniest fingernail, in the same spot on each bag. When Dimitri's cousin Ivan walked through the room, the men at his table attended to their tasks with a renewed zeal and concentration. Everyone at the office spoke Russian, and everyone seemed afraid of Ivan. Yuri explained to Aleks one morning how they'd all recently arrived in Berlin with Ivan's help to escape the crazy inflation, lack of jobs, and the mafia's reign back in Russia. They all needed to work off the cost of their German paperwork, which Ivan had offered to take care of for them.

The square windowpanes next to Aleks' chair looked

out on rooftops and the sky over Berlin. Cumulus clouds, plump and buoyant, arranged themselves in layers against the sky just as they did in Moscow. About this time last year, he'd walked from the tram stop to the orchestra's rehearsal hall and stopped to admire an endless blue sky and the perfect white clouds levitating over Moscow. He'd felt time's push and all the forces outside his control in the days preceding winter's arrival. Those clouds were the last of the mild weather, the last days of strolling with an unbuttoned coat, the last days of seeing the sun every morning. He didn't miss Moscow's deep freeze, but he missed the cramped warmth in the apartment he shared with his mother. He missed the familiarity of his uncle's place, the sharp smell of his aunt's borscht on the stove. Did his mother think something terrible had happened when he didn't return on the train to Moscow? He hoped she wasn't too worried. He hoped his postcard would soothe her fears.

Tatiana came around their workspace with her tray, first stopping at the table on the far side of the room to deliver lunch plates. She wore simple Soviet clothes in greys and browns. She had started serving Aleks last, so the two of them could talk for a few minutes without the other men growing impatient for their food.

Her brown eyes radiated warmth and the corners of her thin lips turned up slightly as she placed the tray down beside Aleks, setting a plate, a glass, and utensils in front of him. She tucked a napkin under his fork with care. The smell of warm food and the kindness in her smile made his days bearable. He wanted to rescue her from this place. Maybe the two of them could set out on their own in Berlin. Surely, they could find jobs and a place to live. It couldn't be that difficult in the West with so many opportunities and so much wealth.

"And how was the preparation this morning?" Aleks asked.

"Today was better. Nina didn't try to steal the butter." She smiled shyly, covering her mouth with her hand. Her eyes met his briefly and then darted toward the floor.

From Tatiana's stories, Aleks had learned there were five or six other girls like her working in the kitchen, preparing lunches and fetching coffees for Ivan and the other men.

She wiped up a few crumbs off the table with a rag and with the other hand, slid a scrap of paper under his napkin. Her move shook him. He flinched with joy. Their eyes met for one electric second and then she turned to leave, waving over her shoulder and tucking the rag back into the white apron wrapped tight around her slim waist.

All the other men in the room were focused on the plates in front of them, so Aleks unfolded the piece of paper in his lap. In pencil, Tatiana had scribbled:

Audition for cello

17 October, 9:00

Potsdamer Strasse 58

Hope welled up in his chest at the same moment the weight of his obligation to Ivan became an unbearable heaviness. He had to leave.

*

Aleks sat on a bench in the hallway, his cello case by his side. The ease and confidence of the other musicians around him meant they were Westerners. Their posture, the keen focus of their gaze, their rosy complexions—everything about them radiated entitlement. Decades of comfort yielded expectations. The air softened around them. They rested on the bench with a lightness Aleks hadn't known existed until a couple months ago when he arrived in Berlin.

Aleks focused on his hands in his lap. He bent his fingers and then lengthened them, stretching the ligaments. He hadn't played in almost a month, since he'd been working at Ivan's warehouse, but he trusted these hands to remember. The crease along the top of his left shoe threatened to split at any moment. The sneakers Ivan had bought him seemed so informal, so he wore his Soviet shoes for the audition. He didn't want to look like he'd just come off the rugby field. But now he regretted this decision.

The other musicians sitting on the simple wooden bench appeared about the same age as Aleks—around twenty-five—but they wore jeans with worn knees and unraveling hems. The woman to his right sported a silver ring in her nose. Another guy further down had the sides of his head shaved and longer hairs in the middle stuck out in all directions. Surely, Aleks re-assured himself, the other musicians had less experience and less formal training.

He felt the wall behind his back and the solid bench beneath him and told himself over and over that he would be okay. Breathe in, breathe out. He had arrived ten minutes late and out of breath. He'd had no money for his subway ticket, so every time he spotted anyone official-looking during the thirty-minute journey, every muscle in his body clenched tight with fear. His dress shirt still clung to his damp armpits. Breathe in, breathe out.

He'd risen early that morning, before Ivan and Dimitri woke up. He'd moved around the apartment silently, like a ghost, getting dressed, hoisting his cello out of the closet and slipping into his shoes.

The night before, Ivan had gotten angry about an empty milk carton. Aleks had poured himself a glass of milk before bed, and Ivan had flown into a rage, his face contorted.

'The carton is empty," Ivan had said, shaking the carton as tiny droplets of milk splattered everywhere.

"It's empty?" Dimitri said, now standing by Ivan's side, his arms crossed. "There won't be milk for breakfast, Aleks."

Milk was plentiful in Berlin. They simply had to go to the store and buy more. They didn't need ration cards. The store wouldn't run out of milk. Maybe Aleks would get this audition and then he could move into an apartment of his own. Maybe he and Tatiana could live there together.

Sitting on the bench, his cello case leaning against his leg, Aleks tried to pinpoint the moment when Dimitri's family bond with Ivan eclipsed his friendship with Aleks. Was it before they even left the orchestra's farewell party at the Hotel Ambassador that night and slipped into Ivan's car? Or was it once Ivan bought them clothes? Or maybe since they started working in Ivan's warehouse?

The door opened and a young man in a black leather motorcycle jacket exited with a cello case over his shoulder. How could the judges take this man seriously as a musician when he looked like a rebellious teenager? Aleks regretted wearing his dress shirt and realized he should have worn the jeans Ivan had bought him. A young woman in bell-bottoms stood in the doorway and read from a sheet of paper in her hand. "Knuttel," she said. The woman with the nose ring stood up from the bench and disappeared into the room with her violin, the door clicking behind her.

By now, surely Aleks' mother had received his postcard of Berlin's TV tower shining against a blue sky and his belated birthday greeting. He imagined her holding the card in her hands, a tear running down her cheek and then clutching the card to her chest. Did she sleep with the card under her pillow? Did she wish and wait for his return? Would she ever forgive him?

The door opened and the woman exited the audition with her violin. The woman in bell-bottoms appeared in the doorway and read Aleks' name from the paper in her hands. Anxiety blossomed in his chest. He stood and followed her inside.

The judges were so young. In Russia, a committee of elders, lifelong musicians, always made any decisions about a musician's talent. Aleks sat down in a chair in front of the long table where the judges relaxed in between auditions, chatting amongst themselves or standing up to stretch. A young man in faded jeans stood by the window, gazing out over the rooftops. Aleks made a few adjustments to ensure his strings were tight enough. He rotated his head to loosen up his neck. It had been years since he'd auditioned for a part. His neck and shoulders had hardened into monuments that morning. He took a deep breath. He hadn't played his cello in weeks. He would be fine. The judges found their seats and gave him a nod.

Aleks inhaled, and then he jumped off the cliff, trusting the music would catch him, trusting the momentum of Rachmaninov's cello sonata would keep him afloat. The first movement started slowly, but as the tempo picked up, Aleks was always trying to catch up, like he was one step behind, and he couldn't find his own rhythm. And then his awareness of this lack took his mind and energy away from the music, so he fell further behind, and his struggle to catch up made a mockery of the piece. For a moment, a voice in his head told him to stop and ask the judges if he could start over, but he was already more than halfway through, so he ignored the voice and kept going.

The friction of his bow on the strings sent each note's vibration through his hand, up his arm and into his chest. He quivered and shook with the music's ferocity. He chased after something he couldn't find, and when it was all over, he leaned back in his chair, exhausted. He hadn't played in so long. His muscles had forgotten. A sense of shame settled over him.

His breath calmed, and he gradually returned to the room. The row of judges avoided his eyes, busy scribbling notes on the papers in front of them. Aleks placed his cello back in its case and snapped the buckles in place. He wanted to disappear, evaporate in an instant. He stood to leave, and one of the judges, a young guy with a single, dark eyebrow, approached Aleks.

But Aleks avoided hearing what he had to say. All the air had left the room and he needed to escape. Aleks backed towards the door, saying "goodbye" and "thank you" in Russian, and then turned and stepped into the hallway. Embarrassment quickened his pace past the other musicians with their wild hairstyles and their confidence. Despair shuttled him out the door and down the stairs. Music had always been the one thing he could count on in his life. Now, it seemed even that constancy had left him. In over a decade, he had never gone more than a few days without playing his cello and now he understood why.

Once outside, the wind picked up and a grey November sky threatened rain. A gust scattered a cluster of yellow leaves across the sidewalk. Aleks stepped on one and it crunched underfoot. He had to ride the subway back to Charlottenburg without a ticket once again. Maybe the police would catch him this time and lock him up. He deserved it. He stopped at the crosswalk and waited for the signal to turn green.

A dark cloud over Berlin sent raindrops down, tapping at his Soviet coat. As he crossed the intersection, the raindrops increased their tempo, and once he reached the other side, the grey sky released a shower. He wrapped his arms around his cello case, cradling the instrument, and headed for the overhang of an office building. Cars glided by on the slick street. Pedestrians scurried, raising umbrellas up to the sky or holding newspapers over their heads.

Aleks gave in to the storm and sat down on a bench underneath the building's overhang. Cigarette butts littered the ground at his feet and, at the end of the bench, an enormous concrete ashtray yawned open, like a sandy mouth full of spongey, yellowed teeth. He unfastened his case and took out his cello. He would have to wait out the storm. Even sprinting three blocks to the subway station would expose his cello to the rain.

He pulled up the collar of his coat to keep out the day's bluster. Pedestrians made valiant leaps across puddles. The city's beige double-decker buses skimmed across the watery thoroughfare. Boxy cars battled the elements, frantic windshield wipers trying to keep up with the downpour. And Aleks felt like he could be anywhere. This same scene could unfold in Moscow. Aleks ran his bow across the strings. And then he knew Bach was right for the moment, for stormy weather.

He played one of Bach's cello sonatas, a little hesitant and unsure, and then immediately moved into another. The day's humidity made his bow sluggish, but gradually, he let go of his fear and lost himself in the music. He found his stride. He didn't worry about pleasing anyone. There were no judges watching him. He played for the joy of the music. He played for the rain.

Occasionally, he heard a clink sound, but he focused on his music. He felt Bach's notes reverberate throughout his body, down his limbs, out to his hands and back into his cello. One with the music, his displacement no longer mattered. His inability to communicate in German didn't matter. His deteriorating friendship with Dimitri didn't matter, his longing for Tatiana didn't matter. Anything that really mattered came out in his music. Clink.

When he came to the end of the piece, Aleks paused for a moment. The rain had quieted and the sun offered warmth. Opening his eyes, sunlight reflected off puddles and the rain-slicked cars traveling down the street. People congregated around Aleks, leaning against the side of the building or standing on the small patch of green between the office building and the sidewalk. Some men stood smoking in their dress shirts and ties, while passersby carrying bags full of groceries or schoolbooks paused on their way somewhere else. Copper and nickel-colored coins fanned out in all directions on the concrete at his feet, and Aleks wondered why his small audience would assume all this beauty was for money.

*

That evening, Aleks placed a jug of milk in the refrigerator next to the small white cartons adorned with red pagodas. Ivan and Dimitri slurped down noodles in silence, steam rising out of similar white cartons on the kitchen table. Aleks could feel the weight of their eyes as he removed the piece of sausage and the half-loaf of bread from his coat pockets. He found a clean plate in the cupboard and unwrapped the sausage, freeing it from the butcher's white paper, and sliced off a piece of bread. His metal knife hitting the ceramic plate punctuated the silence. He sat down on a chair next to Dimitri and covered the piece of dark bread with slim discs of pink sausage. He took a bite and it was the most delicious food he'd eaten in a long time.

When he'd pressed the buzzer at the building's front door ten minutes earlier, Aleks had heard the panic in Ivan's *hello?* Uncertainty and fear were things he'd never detected in his usually booming and confident voice. Holding the door to his apartment open, Ivan had stepped out of the way to allow Aleks to enter with his cello, but as soon as the door closed behind him, Ivan had struck Aleks across the face.

"You fool," Ivan had said. "If they trace you back to me, my entire business could disappear in an instant."

"You put all of us in danger," Dimitri had said, standing behind Ivan.

Aleks sliced off another piece of bread, carved a few slivers of sausage and placed the delicate pink spheres across the bread. His cheek still stung from Ivan's blow, but he ignored the ache in his jaw and ground up each bite of bread and sausage with his teeth before swallowing.

"You only think of yourself," Ivan said, a piece of noodle stuck to his chin. "What if the police had stopped you and asked for your papers? What if the police caught you for riding without a ticket? To be so selfish after all I've done for you!"

"You keep a man prisoner and he will try to break free," Aleks said.

Ivan dropped his fork.

"Prison?" Ivan turned toward Dimitri sitting next to him. "Do you feel like you're in prison?"

"No, Ivan," Dimitri shook his head. "Of course, I appreciate your generosity."

Aleks could smell fear on Dimitri and this filled him with sorrow. Chewing the bread and sausage he'd bought, after he spent the day on his own, going to places he chose and doing what he wanted, Aleks realized he would be all right in Berlin.

No matter what happened, he would survive. And his sore jaw told him he was a threat to Ivan, which felt like a small victory.

When he told Ivan and Dimitri about how he'd sat in front of a building and played his cello and total strangers tossed coins at him, Dimitri looked down at his noodles, avoiding Aleks' gaze.

"You're like the grandmothers on the streets of Moscow, hoping others will take pity and toss a few kopecks their way," Ivan said. He slurped a noodle and wiped off his face with the back of his hand. "Those Germans probably felt sorry for you. That's why they gave you so much money."

Aleks cut more slices of sausage and piled them up on a new piece of bread. He didn't get that feeling. His audience enjoyed his music. He could feel their attention on him. He could feel the music moving through the crowd. His music slowed time, softened the city's sharp edges. Aleks enjoyed the experience. It was different from playing in a concert hall, where there was a great distance between the musicians and their audience. From his bench, people's faces were clear to him, and they expressed a mix of joy and sorrow. The music transported all of them to a different place, a place where all humans were all the same and there were no language barriers or visas or borders.

<u>EXCERPT</u> Magazine No. 1

CONTRIBUTORS

Matthew Binder is the author of the novels *Pure Cosmos Club, The Absolved,* and *High in the Streets.* He is also a primary member of the recording project Bang Bang Jet Away.

Synopsis: *Pure Cosmos Club* tells the story of Paul, an artist whose girlfriend has left him for a surgeon after Paul is fired from yet another day job. Desperate, Paul and his companion, a disabled terrier-mix dog named Blanche, move into the studio space he rents from Danny, the eccentric son of a billionaire hedge fund manager. It's not long before Paul then succumbs to James, a new-age guru he meets at Danny's family mansion in the Hamptons, and enters James' cult, the Pure Cosmos Club. Yet every time Paul believes he's ready for the "Ultimate Level," James raises the price of entry. Just how far will Paul go to attain cosmic oneness?

Pure Cosmos Club will be published by Stalking Horse Press in May 2023. It is now available for pre-order at stalkinghorsepress. com.

*

Ayla Zuraw-Friedland is a writer and publishing professional living in Brooklyn. Her past writing has been published or is forthcoming in The Drift, The London Review of Books, GAY the Magazine, Publisher's Weekly, and The Cape Cod Poetry Review. Twitter: @kaylasansk

Synopsis: *Like Anywhere Else* is the story of Saudade, the Seventh City of Refuge. Here, those who have accidentally caused someone's death can seek protection, healing, and community with others who share this experience without fear of retribution. Told in alternating perspectives, we follow the lives of Ariel, a 13 year old boy who became the first resident of Saudade, Cora, a triplet who believes she was sent to Saudade in error; and You, the unnamed narrator, who finds themselves in Saudade after a car accident. Though the city initially seems like a utopia, an impending refugee crisis reveals the ways in which the residents are prone to the evils and secrecy of the outside world even in the midst of their own second chances.

CONTRIBUTORS

Rebecca Pyle's fiction appears in many art/literary journals, including Map Literary, Pangyrus, Guesthouse, The Hong Kong Review, Gargoyle Magazine, BarBar, The Lindenwood Review, Eclectica, and Posit. She recently won the 2022 Miracle Monocle Award for Creative Writing, and, once upon a time, while living in London, shared a first prize purse in the United Kingdom's National Poetry Competition with the Irish poet Medbhe McGuckian. Rebecca is also a visual artist, her artwork appearing in dozens of art/literary journals or on their covers. See rebeccapyleartist.com.

Synopsis: *Time for a Chocolate* is a novel about men in England, father and sons, all searching for a mother or the ghost of a mother. Young James' American mother is dead, and he is daring enough to leave America and survive in the country she loved, England. At the age of twelve, he improbably succeeds in proving himself the rightful heir of his English father's estate in Bloomsbury. Not weighted by a student's usual worries, James decides he will travel much further than England in his mind: he will become a science fiction author. James, like his father, never marries, but adopts two sons. Unlike James, who came to try to right the wrongs done to his mother, they seek their sad living mothers, for whom they also cannot make much at all, really, come out right. It is too late.

*

James Reich is a novelist, essayist, and journalist from England, now a resident of Santa Fe, New Mexico. In addition to *The Moth for the Star*, his most recent novels are the science fiction *The Song My Enemies Sing*, the doppelganger noir *Soft Invasions*, and *Mistah Kurtz! A Prelude to Hear of Darkness* (Anti-Oedipus Press). James is a contributor to SPIN Magazine, and others. www.jamesreich-books.com

Synopsis: *The Moth for the Star* (7.13 Books, September 2023) is a dark, sprawling romance, a late-modern 'satanic Gatsby.' Charles Varnas is a murderer who cannot recall his victim. His cool, androgynous conspirator Campbell may hold the secret. Haunted and dissolute, they struggle to come to terms with the psychic weight of their crime.

Garth Miró is a writer based in New York City. His work has appeared in Litro, Sundog Lit, XRAY, and Maudlin House among others. His debut novel *The Vacation* is out now through Expat Press. He works as a handyman.

Synopsis for *The Vacation*: Hugo wants to destroy his life. He's worked long enough. Where better to fry than on a shimmering, sunny, subtropical cruise? A ship that takes vacations seriously—worships them. Maybe there Hugo can finally relax like he's always wanted, *forever*.

*

Sara Doty received her Master of Fine Arts in creative writing from Stetson University in 2022. She is a United States Marine Corps veteran. She writes fiction and poetry.

Synopsis for *The Wilds*: Sam wants to live out the rest of her life in the Wilds, a place we call Florida and Sam calls sanctum, but she can never stay on the peninsula for too long. The ghost of her sister haunts her, and something else follows Sam too, something she fears she will not outrun. After the death of her mother Sam begins to understand the Wilds on a biological level, and her connection to the peninsula is reveled.

*

David Luntz's work is forthcoming or appeared in Pithead Chapel, Vestal Review, Reflex Press, Scrawl Place, Best Small Fictions (2021), trampset, X-R-A-Y Lit, Fiction International, Janus Literary, Orca Lit, Rejection Letters, Atticus Review, Heavy Feather Review among others.

Synopsis for *Crocodile Man*: When Jimmy, a freelance hitman and bibliophile, is hired to transport an unknown package across Los Angeles, he stumbles into a child-trafficking ring. He finds himself on the run from the cartel with a boy who knows too much. The cartel brings in their most vicious enforcer "Torquemada" to track them down, and Jimmy must use all his skills to evade him, save the boy, and destroy the trafficking ring.

CONTRIBUTORS

Valerie Palmer was born in Washington, DC and now lives in Los Angeles. *The Brightest Flames* is her first novel.

Synopsis: *The Brightest Flames* is a literary novel set in the heady days of early-90s Berlin. When Sam, an American, is fired from her au pair job in a posh suburb of Berlin, she takes refuge at a squat in Berlin's Kreuzberg neighborhood rather than return home to the U.S. She is immediately drawn to Fritz, a German, but he is more concerned with Berlin's neo-Nazi problem, gentrification in a post-Wall Berlin and an influx of refugees from the East. Aleks, a Russian, arrives at the squat with only his cello and a dream to play in one of Berlin's prestigious orchestras, but he must busk in order to eat. These characters struggle with love, idealism, poverty and danger, all while the story builds toward a heartbreaking tragedy.

CPSIA information can be obtained
at www.ICGtesting.com
Printed in the USA
BVHW081941090323
660095BV00007B/553